SOURCE BOOKS ON EDUCATION

1. Bilingual Education: *A Source Book for Educators*
    by Alba N. Ambert and Sarah Melendez

2. Reading and Study Skills in the Secondary Schools: *A Source Book*
    by Joyce N. French

3. Creating Connections: *Books, Kits, and Games for Children*
    by Betty P. Cleaver, Barbara Chatton, and Shirley Vittum Morrison

4. Gifted, Talented, and Creative Young People: *A Guide to Theory, Teaching, and Research*
    by Morris I. Stein

5. Teaching Science to Young Children: *A Resource Book*
    by Mary D. Iatridis

6. Microcomputers and Social Studies: *A Resource Guide for the Middle and Secondary Grades*
    by Joseph A. Braun, Jr.

7. Special Education: *A Source Book*
    by Manny Sternlicht

8. Computers in the Classroom . . . What Shall I Do?: *A Guide*
    by Walter Burke

9. Learning to Read and Write: The Role of Language Acquisition and Aesthetic Development, *A Resource Guide*
    by Ellen J. Brooks

10. School Play: *A Source Book*
    by James H. Block and Nancy R. King

11. Computer Simulations: *A Source Book to Learning in an Electronic Environment*
    by Jerry Willis, Larry Hovey, and Kathleen Hovey

12. Day Care: *A Source Book*
    by Kathleen Pullan Watkins and Lucius Durant, Jr.

13. Project Head Start: Past, Present, and Future Trends in the Context of Family Needs
    by Valora Washington and Ura Jean Oyemade

14. Adult Literacy: *A Source Book and Guide*
    by Joyce French

15. Mathematics Education in Secondary Schools and Two-Year Colleges: *A Source Book*
    by Louise S. Grinstein and Paul J. Campbell

16. Black Children and American Institutions: *An Ecological Review and Resource Guide*
    by Valora Washington and Velma LaPoint

17. Resources for Educational Equity: *A Source Book for Grades Pre-Kindergarten–12*
    by Merle Froschl and Barbara Sprung

18. Multicultural Education: *A Source Book*
    by Patricia G. Ramsey, Edwina Battle Vold, and Leslie R. Williams

19. Sexuality Education: *A Resource Book*
    by Carol Cassell and Pamela M. Wilson

20. Reforming Teacher Education *Issues and New Directions*
    edited by Joseph A. Braun, Jr.

21. Educational Technology: *A Planning and Resource Guide Supporting Curriculum*
    by James E. Eisele and Mary Ellin Eisele

EDUCATIONAL TECHNOLOGY

SOURCE BOOKS ON EDUCATION
(VOL. 21)

GARLAND REFERENCE LIBRARY
OF SOCIAL SCIENCE
(VOL. 372)

EDUCATIONAL TECHNOLOGY
A Planning and Resource Guide
Supporting Curriculum

James E. Eisele

Mary Ellin Eisele

GARLAND PUBLISHING, INC. • NEW YORK & LONDON
1990

Library of Congress Cataloging-in-Publication Data

Eisele, James E.
   Educational technology: a planning and resource guide supporting
curriculum / James E. Eisele, Mary Ellin Eisele.
      p.   cm. — (Garland reference library of social science; vol.
372. Source books on education; vol. 21)
      ISBN 0-8240-8549-3 (alk. paper)
      1. Educational technology—United States—Handbooks, manuals, etc.
I. Eisele, Mary Ellin. II. Title. III. Series: Garland reference
library of social science; vol. 372. IV. Series: Garland reference
library of social science. Source books on education; vol. 21.
LB1028.3.E426   1990
371.3'078—dc20   89-78108
                                                                CIP

Printed on acid-free, 250-year-life paper
Manufactured in the United States of America

To my family

..........and to your memory, Jim

Contents

Acknowledgments

We would like to express our appreciation to the individuals who either assisted or supported in the development and writing of this book: Charles Connor for his contributions to the original manuscript, Steve Preston and Jane Lee for their inspiration to write the book, and Vicky Bowen, who provided assistance with collecting materials and resources.

Many thanks also, to Lutian Wootton, John Reynolds, Michael Waugh, Thomas Reeves, Bob Hart, Nancy Hart and Gerald Firth.

Special thanks to C. Thomas Holmes and to Alphonse Buccino, Dean of the College of Education, The University of Georgia.

Introduction

This book was written for the person who is interested in learning about and using technology in schools or other settings which have an educational or training mission. It is "learner friendly", in that the interested learner will find ideas, definitions, descriptions and applications understandable and meaningful. It is a guide in the most helpful sense of the word, in that the learner is given *criteria* rather than rules, for making decisions. And it is timely.

In 1985, a report from the U.S. Office of Education predicted that educational technology would lead to the transformation of the public schools. Holden (1989) points out that nowhere can the estimated 1.5 million computers in public schools be said to have "transformed education." She might have used "technology" in place of computers, when she wrote further, "These many years into the computer age, teachers still have little training in computer use, much less how to choose and employ software productively (pp. 906-907)." Turner (1989) reported that the U.S. Office of Technology Assessment cited the need for teachers to have "both training and education if technology is to take hold (p. A9)."

Equity - or inequity - of access to educational technology has been a significant factor in the delayed "coming of age." Females, as a group, have been left out of the mainstream of technology use, as have Hispanics and blacks (LaPointe & Martinez, 1988, p. 60). Failure to address the restraints which, apparent and real, keep females away from technology results in a two-edged sword, since women comprise the majority gender of teachers, who are therefore, not computer-competent.

The purposes of this book are: to enable the reader to learn about technology, to enable the reader to learn how technology *has* been used and therefore stimulate ideas for more effective use and application, and to enable the reader to gain the knowledge and skills to *effectively* plan and implement programs for using and managing educational technology. For example, it provides the background and aids necessary to implement technological solutions to educational problems, whether the problems are instructional or administrative.

Whether the reader is just getting started or is experienced with educational technology, this book will present the information necessary to build knowledge, acquire skills, and function effectively.

Part I gives an overview of educational technology today. In this section a definition of educational technology is presented, and the reader is introduced to several major concepts and terms needed to understand what technology is, how it can help, and how to use it. A systematic approach to the utilization of technology is advocated, and Part One provides background knowledge for making these kinds of informed decisions. The novice should read this part with great care before proceeding to Part II.

Part II contains information and aids as well as a step-by-step process for planning, developing, and implementing programs in educational technology. Each step in the process is discussed for understanding, and aids for carrying out each step are provided. The process described encourages innovation and diffusion in any program, product, or process in education.

Part III provides a broad spectrum of supplementary resources. It contains a collection of additional resources which have been found to be especially informative for understanding the processes, or useful for carrying them out. These resources include checklists, evaluative criteria, articles, guidelines, and some alternatives to procedures discussed in Part II.

Careful reading and use of this book should result in the reader's ability to do the following:

1. To systematically create a plan for the use of educational technology in schools or other settings.

2. To make decisions about hardware, software, logistics, and competencies needed for successful use of educational technology.

3. To use educational technology to improve educational performance.

4. To evaluate progress in planning for and implementing educational technology in schools or other organizations.

Notes

Holden, Constance. "Computers Make Slow Progress in Class." *Science* 244no.26(May 1989):906-909.

LaPointe, Archie and Michael Martinez. "Aims, Equity and Access in Computer Education." *Phi Delta Kappan* 70no.1(Sept 88):59-61.

Turner, Judith Axler. "Teacher Training Colleges' Slow Move to Computers Blamed for Schools' Lag in Integrating Technology." *Chronicle of Higher Education* 35no.45(Jul 19, 1989): A9-A11.

Suggested Reading

Damarin, Suzanne K. "Re-thinking Equity: An Imperative for Educational Computing." *The Computing Teacher* 16no.7(April 1989):16-18.

Part I

Chapter 1
Overview of Educational Technology

The purpose of this chapter is to introduce the reader to the field of educational technology. A comprehensive definition of educational technology will be developed and suggested as a sound basis for planning and managing technology. In addition, this chapter explores the nature of current technology, both the products and the processes, used in education and training. A rationale for technology is discussed and established based upon two recognized needs in education, the need for improvement, and the need for accountability.

Defining Technology

Traditionally, technology has been defined as the application of science to the improvement of the human condition. Pure science seeks knowledge for its own sake; technology seeks to apply science to practical human endeavors for the benefit of people. Science is knowing and the pursuit of knowing. Technology is doing and the pursuit of effective and efficient ways of doing.

If the definition of technology as "doing and the pursuit of ways of doing" is accepted, then technology can be viewed as the use of both the process of doing and the products developed for doing it. This definition eliminates the dichotomy between process and product which is sometimes encountered in writing and discussions about technology.

Defining Educational Technology

Educational technology has especially been afflicted with misunderstandings about its nature. Many people would associate educational technology with audiovisual materials. Others would see it as computer-based education. Others might see educational technology as the application of the systems approach to teaching and learning. Educational technology is all of those things, and more. Many authors have written about educational technology, but none offer a more eloquent definition than that reported to the President and Congress of the United States in 1970 (19):

> Instructional technology can be defined in two ways. In its more familiar sense, it means the media born of the communications revolution which can be used for instructional purposes alongside the teacher, textbook, and blackboard... The second and less familiar definition of instructional technology goes beyond any particular medium or device. In this sense, instructional technology is more than the sum of its parts. It is a systematic way of designing, carrying out, and evaluating the total process of learning and teaching in terms of specific objectives, based on research in human learning and communications, and employing a combination of human and nonhuman resources to bring about more effective instruction.

Illustration 1 depicts the view of technology and problem solving as described above by the Commission Report.

The word "educational" in educational technology means that the technology being applied is for the purpose of improving human factors related to education. This is, indeed, a broad area which may include everything from teaching and learning to the scheduling of school buses. However, the bus schedule is not really integral to education and, therefore, the term is used here to refer only to the major educational tasks of teaching and learning and other directly related tasks.

"Education" is defined here as all of the activities and opportunities offered to learners for the facilitation of learning. This definition of education narrows the focus of the book to only those activities which

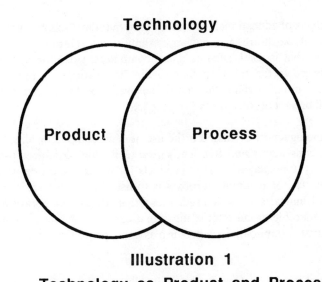

Illustration 1
Technology as Product and Process

directly affect learning, but includes many management operations as well as direct instructional functions.

Educational Technology in the Schools

There is little doubt that technology has found its way into the schools and the educational lives of many people. Virtually every school in America currently has access to a wide range of educational technologies. (For example, latest reports indicate over 1.5 million microcomputers in schools in the U.S.) Further, since the introduction of microcomputers in the marketplace, the acceleration of hardware and software acquisition has been significant. Rather than encouraging the continued acquisition of hardware and software, the authors advocate slowing down the pace in order to ensure the time for careful analysis and planning for the use of appropriate technologies which reflect the definition of technology as both product and process.

Educational Technology as Products in the Schools

The products of educational technology used in today's schools include a variety of hardware and software applications. Hardware is the equipment that is used, such as micro-computers, videodisc systems, etc. Software is the term applied to the "instructions," commands, directions, and programs that make hardware perform operations. More will be said of software in Chapter 5.

The technology most discussed is the use of microcomputers, although the most consistently and frequently *used* technology continues to be printed text. One way to classify products for use in education which may be useful for planning purposes is to list those which are rather traditional and already well used, those that are contemporary and hold considerable promise for immediate use, and those that are some-what futuristic, but hold much promise as appropriate technologies for education.

Traditional Products	Contemporary Products	Future ?? Products
movie film	*microcomputers	voice control
slides/filmstrips	*main-frame computers	televideo
projections	*modems	advanced networks
charts/pictures/graphs	*telecommunications	knowledge bases
television	*electronic bulletin	laser
printed/programmed text	boards	advanced
	*voice synthesizer	supercomputers
	*optical discs	I-CAI (Interactive
	*videodiscs	Computer Aided
	*interactive video	Instruction)
	*CD ROM	
	*CD-I	

* Indicates terms which are explained in Chapter 3.

Illustration 2
Classifications for Planning Purposes

There are other available technologies and many more on the horizon to be developed. Many of these products are currently available and ready to use. Of course, a purpose of this book is to promote careful planning, and that is what must be done in order to take advantage of available technology.

Technology seems to *beg* not the question of "can it be used?", but , "should it be used?" Technology *can* be used — but *should* it be used? If so, when and under what conditions? To answer the latter question, consider these criteria for using a given technology:

1. Is it appropriate for the goals and objectives of the school?
2. Is it appropriate for the target learning population?
3. Is the hardware available?
4. Is the software available?
5. Can software be adapted and/or created easily?
6. Is the hardware easy to use?
7. Is the software easy to use?
8. Is the "system" feasible in the situation?
9. Is the "system" flexible?

Educational Technology as Process in Education

The second definition of educational technology, described earlier in the chapter, deals with a larger view of technology other than product development, though it also includes a great concern for such development. This definition refers to the entire process of planning, development, implementation, and evaluation as a *systematic* process. This book advocates such a systematic approach to the utilization of technology, with Part I providing background knowledge for making decisions and Part II providing the format and aids for using a systematic approach.

Technology, as process, involves the use of tools and resources to *systematically* plan, develop, implement, and evaluate any change or change process. There are several tools available to guide the systematic process, or the managers and participants of any planning team may create their own tool, perhaps using a variation of one of the following:

Program Evaluation Review Technique (PERT)
Program Planning, Budgeting, and Evaluation System (PPBES)
Critical Path Method (CPM)
Hierarchical Input, Process, Output analysis (HIPO)
Systems Analysis
Cost Effectiveness Analysis
Performance Task Analysis
Front-end Analysis

The approach used in this book is meant to be systematically applied. There is no reason, however, why it might not be altered somewhat to suit the specific situation in which it is being applied. This approach will first be presented in Chapter 5 and then applied throughout the remainder of the book.

To use technology in the schools also should include the use of technology as an *object* of instruction. Therefore, in Chapter 3, teaching both the products and the processes of educational technology are discussed.

The Need for Educational Technology

The proliferation of technology in schools is considerable. We have even suggested that the pace of acquiring hardware and software for education be somewhat slowed to allow time for more systematic planning. The first question which needs to be raised is, "Does education need technology?" If the answer is "yes", then the next question should be, "What should technology be used for?", and then, "Which technologies should be used?"

Does Education Need Technology?

Many, but not all, educators and parents would argue strongly that education does, in fact, need technology as an object of instruction as part of the curriculum, as a tool for use by teachers and administrators, and as an aid for learning. Those who would argue for the need for technology in education would probably suggest that the need exists because of the continuous search for improvement and because of the demand for accountability.

The Need for Improvement

Education, like most human ventures, always seems to be in pursuit of improvement. The need for change, the desire for improvement, and a discomfort with what exists seems to always be in the air. This seems to be true in almost every aspect of life, including education. In the fashion world, a popular style of clothing may last for 1 to 5 years. With automobiles, the lifespan of a particular style may be from 1 to 3 years. On television, shows sometimes last 2 or 3 months, or less. In education, major reform movements come along about every 3 to 5 years. All of these changes would appear to have a common basis: humans are never satisfied with the status quo; they are always looking for something better. As Goodlad so wrote in discussing curriculum changes:

Curriculum change usually stems from assumed excesses or inadequacies in what exists. A period of change produces its own shortcomings and creates the need for another (Goodlad, 1967, p. 5).

If there is a dissatisfaction with what exists in education, which would appear to be the case, then the search for a *better* way may be an important pursuit. Furthermore, the history of human civilization is characterized by humans searching for *"the better way."* The search for improvement is a natural process which predetermines the need for change. But does that mean a concomitant need for technology in education?

Some educators and scientists believe that the use of technology in education is needed. Skinner (1953, p. 5), for example, suggests that the enormously successful "methods of science" be applied to human affairs. In the years since 1953, considerable effort to do so has been reported.

The search for new learning resources proceeds with increased vigor and speed. The success of improving production in business, industry, agriculture, and medicine through applications of technology, stirs the hopes of teachers, school administrators, and citizens generally that similar improvements can take place in teaching and learning (Trow, 1963, iii).

Thus, the constant search for improvement, which seems ever present, strongly suggests the need for technology in education. How else can significant changes be brought about in this day and age? At least, this is one compelling argument for its use.

The Need for Accountability

If the demand for change, which often comes from within education, is not a sufficient argument for increased use of technology, the demand of the community, of parents, business leaders, government officials, and educational reformers to include technology in education requires educators' close attention. School principals often report great pressure from their communities to include technology in the curriculum and as working tools for their students. Newspapers, journals, and television tout the need for improved learning *about* technology in the schools. The report by the National Commission on Excellence in Education entitled, *A Nation at Risk : The Imperative for Educational Reform* (1983), recommends both the inclusion of computer science in the curriculum and the use of technology for the development of instructional materials.

Although his topic was educational technology in the state of Utah, Moss's (1988) evaluation is germane to the entire American educational scene:

> Technology is not the sole solution to the challenge confronting education.... But without it, no other solution will be entirely successful (pp. 25-26).

Clearly, there is a reason, if not a dire need, to expand and improve the use of technology in education. Still, the cautionary note to proceed carefully and systematically remains very much in order because:

> **technology can be an extremely successful way of doing something that should never have been done in the first place.**

Summary

This chapter presents a working definition of educational technology, an overview of what kinds of technology are currently available, and a list of possible future developments in technology. Criteria for deciding whether to use a particular technology are given, as well as a list of "tools" or techniques to guide the systematic selection process. The relationship between the use of technology and the need for improvement and accountability in education is discussed.

References

Commission on Instructional Technology. *To Improve Learning.* Washington:U.S. Government Printing Office, 1970.

Goodlad, John I. "Essay One,The Curriculum" in *Rational Planning of Curriculum and Instruction,* by National Education Association. Washington: The Association, 1967.

Holden, Constance. "Computers Make Slow Progress in Class." *Science* 244(May 26, 1989):906-909.

Jirka, Charles C., and Sharon E. Smaldino. "Computer Assisted Instruction." *Middle School Journal* 20no.4(March 1989):26-28.

The National Commission on Excellence in Education. *A Nation at Risk: The Imperative for Educational Reform.* Washington, D.C.: Government Printing Office, 1983.

Moss, James R. "Utah: A Case Study." *Phi Delta Kappan*, 70 no.1, (September 88):25-26.

Skinner, B.F. *Science and Human Behavior.* New York: the Free Press, 1953.

Trow, William Clark. *Teacher and Technology: New Designs for Learning.* New York: Appleton-Century-Crofts, 1963

Suggested Readings

Cawley, John F. & Jane Y. Murdock. "Technology and Students With Handicaps." *Contemporary Educational Psychology*, 12no.3 (July 1987):212-221.

D'Ignazio, Fred. "Bringing the 1990s to the Classroom of Today." *Phi Delta Kappan* 70no.1(Sept. 1988):26-27.

Edwards, Carol. "Project MiCRO." *The Computing Teacher* 16no.5 (February 1989):11-13.

Knirk, Frederick G., and Kent L. Gustafson. *Instructional Technology* New York:Holt, Rinehart and Winston, 1986.

Melmed, Arthur. "The Technology of Education: Problem and Opportunity." *Technological Horizons in Education* 14 no.2 (Sept 1986):77-81.

Chapter 2
History of Technology in the Schools

The purpose of this chapter is to present an overview of the history of technology in education. The reason for this sojourn into history is two-fold. First, many people think of educational technology as microcomputers in education, with no significant precedents. Hopefully this venture will facilitate a view of the evolutionary nature of the process of using educational technology which has taken place in the past. Knowing of this evolutionary process should also reduce the tendency to apply any single technology to the solution of all problems.

Second, by looking carefully at past events, the history of technology in schools, we may avoid repeating the mistakes and errors of judgment. Knowing what took place in the past might enable us to have a more accurate view of what is occurring today, and facilitate planning for the future. Therefore, this chapter will present some of the highlights in the history of educational technology and will expand on the current era.

The history of technology in education may be thought of as a series of phases, or "revolutions" (Ashby, 1967). Even before written history there was "evidence of primitive communications, technologies in the form of cave drawings and organized languages. These symbolic representational systems were the predecessors of modern educational technology.

Another major phase in the evolution of educational technology was the use of written language to preserve and spread the printed language. Illustrative of this period in education were the horn book, chalkboards, and paper and writing instruments. Soon thereafter came the handwritten manuscripts of important documents such as the Bible. This "revolution," according to (Ashby, 1967), "was the adoption of the written word as the tool of education. Prior to that time, oral instruction prevailed, and it was only with reluctance that writing was permitted to co-exist with the spoken word in the classroom (p.360)."

Yet another phase or revolution in the history of technology in education can be traced to early civilizations when humans first began to formalize their understanding of adult roles and the purposes for teaching these roles to the young. Until that time, the initiation of the young into adulthood was an informal process marked by the immediate family (especially mothers and grandparents) overseeing the development of their children through imitation of adult roles. The shift to differentiation and specialization of adult roles, and the concomitant need for specialized teachers led to another "revolution" when the "task of educating the young was shifted, in part, from parents to teachers and from the home to the school (Ashby, pp. 359-360)."

The third of Ashby's "revolutions" may have had greater impact on education than any previous invention or discovery. This milestone was the invention of the Gutenberg printing machine which came about in the mid-fifteenth century. This single invention, with the subsequent wide availability of books, altered the nature of education so dramatically that its effect is still felt today. Of course, the effect referred to is the dominance of, and heavy reliance upon, textbooks as a basis for most education, curriculum, and instructional procedures.

The fourth phase in the history of the development of educational technology discussed by Ashby is the advent of the use of electronics. This phase began with simple electronics, or electrical devices, such as the electric light bulb, the telegraph, and the telephone, (which) "portended (later) developments in electronics, notably those involving the radio, television, tape recorder, and computer (p. 361)." Calculating machines were built that were reliable, accurate, and much faster than mental operations for calculating.

These inventions and developments set the stage for what might be called the fifth, and latest, revolution in education and educational technology. Developments in communications technology led to considerable use of television in school classrooms, including closed circuit television. This utilization was often criticized for its almost exclusive use of the "talking face" where one teacher was recorded, for later playback, doing what would normally be done in a classroom.

The tendency to use the talking face approach was turned around by the introduction of the children's television production, *Sesame Street*. *Sesame Street* was based upon the science of education as known at the time. It attempted to implement principles such as motivating learners, involvement of learners in instruction, active responding of learners, and feedback to their responses. Clearly, this was a hallmark in the use of television for educational purposes.

About the same time that *Sesame Street* was being televised, much progress was being made in the area of computer technology. The large machines, built during World War II were being made smaller in size and greater in capability. Higher level programming languages (such as Fortran, COBOL, BASIC, PASCAL, and C) were being developed , that made the use of computers far easier. Physical size reductions, and capability increases, were no less than phenomenal, resulting in the personal computers of today.

The development of microcomputers, the personal computers of today, was a landmark, by itself. Developments in photographically reducing large circuitry into micro size, "imprinting" these microcircuits onto silicon, and building powerful microprocessors, was a major advance in computer technology. The application and use of these microcomputers for educational purposes was another. Many individuals, engineers, computer scientists, hobbyists, and hackers are responsible for the creation of microcomputer technology. Two men, Steven Wozniak and Steven Jobs (co-founders of Apple Computer, Incorporated), are worthy of being singled out for their dedication to helping improve education. The efforts of these two men to acquaint educators with microcomputers, to make hardware available at significantly lower prices to educators, and efforts to underwrite and encourage the development of educational software have had a tremendous impact on educational technology as it exists today.

Transporting students, teachers or materials by flying airplanes to and from remote areas became an accepted, though limited practice. Another approach used an airplane flying overhead transmitting programs to large geographical areas. A column in Technology Teacher (p.32), points out that research is currently underway to put a lightweight airplane 60,000 feet above the earth over a city to serve as a communications platform relaying television, radio, cellular telephone, paging service, and data-transmission communications.

The Northwest Report, (1989, pp.1,6) describes distance education as the name given to instruction which takes place " when students and teachers cannot meet face to face. " Distance education "was born as a result of the use of various kinds of technology."

In 1986, Congress passed the Rural Education Initiative. In its first year three "promising techniques using different technological approaches to distance education were identified:

> 1. Television-Television courses take two forms: Long range (satellite) transmission and short range(cable) transmission. Instruction is usually one-way video two-way audio interaction by phone.

> 2. Audiographics-An audiographics system can connect several remote sites with a central classroom, using microcomputers with graphics tablets, modems and speaker phones.

> 3. Computers-Using a combination of print, video, and computer based materials, computer based programs can provide an individualized course of study through electronic mail and on-line testing (p.6)."

The scientific basis of education has made considerable progress. Important contributions to research on teaching and learning have been made by numerous behavioral scientists, educators, and psychologists. Some of those who have been widely recognized for their research in the area during recent years include Jere Brophy, Jerome Bruner, Arthur Combs, Robert Gagne, N. L. Gage, Robert Glaser, John Goodlad, Madelyn Hunter, B. F. Skinner, Hilda Taba, and Ralph Tyler. Of course, these individuals represent only a very small percentage of those who have contributed to the literature from which educators presently draw in the planning, development, implementation, and evaluation of programs utilizing educational technology.

An additional ingredient which may result in the next revolution is the recognition of the importance of implementation and diffusion into practice. Because much of what has been developed has never found its way into the classroom, the need for effective strategies, based upon knowledge of how to bring about change, has been recognized as of vital importance to successful implementation.

Some of the key concepts about creating change which have been discovered and used in recent years are:

1. Individuals expected to implement change should be involved in planning the change.

2. Proposed changes should address the perceived needs of those who must implement change.

3. Individuals who are to participate in the change process should be well aware of the proposed changes and various other alternatives.

4. Communication between "change agents" and participants should be open and clear.

5. The plan for implementation must be systematic, clear, and well documented.

6. Incentives for change must be applied.

7. Change requires monitoring and coaching from peers and leaders.

These recent ideas on change, along with previous and current developments in communications technology, computer technology, and the scientific basis of education offer a greater potential for educational improvement than ever before. New developments in all these areas are taking place even now! In the communications industry, developments include interactive video, satellite telecommunications, laser transmission of audio and video signals, and long-distance networking. Current developments in computer technology include smaller size, larger capacity, increased use of networking, graphics and color (both screen and printed), integrated software to increase capability and convenience and reduce the need to purchase multiple packages for special applications. Other changes are being developed that may not be widely known to the public at this time.

Perhaps most exciting, however, for the educational technologist is the progress being made toward a technology of human performance. This technology is also the product of continuous efforts based on previous ones already discussed. Today's performance technology is one which recognizes the importance of all of the notions discussed above. It is based upon the concepts of knowing the needs for change, analyzing the nature of the needed changes, determining the specific performance requirements needed, and designing instructional strategies to bring about the necessary changes. Harless (1986) describes the process as follows:

First, we ask: "What are your organization's goals?"

Second, "Which of those goals are not currently being met?"

Third, " Who needs to what, when, and how well?"

Fourth, "Is the problem to be corrected a deficiency of: Skill and/or knowledge; Environmental; or Motivational?

Finally, "We develop the performance or instructional technology to teach the skills and/or knowledge needed, seek changes in the environment, or change the incentives."

Developments in all areas continue to move forward as humans continue to search for better ways of doing things. Those developments which most directly influence education include communications, computers, and the scientific basis of education. What is known today, however, seems sufficient to expect that education in the next decade will show major leaps toward more effective educational technologies.

Summary

This chapter has traced the evolution of educational technology through five phases, called "Revolutions" by Eric Ashby (1967). The first revolution removed learners from the family into organized schools, the second occurred with the use of written language as a means of instruction. The third major change came about through the invention of printing machines. The fourth revolution began with relatively modern developments in the field of electronics. Each of these phases was clearly associated with its preceding era. The fifth revolution is at hand, many believe, and it is based upon progress made in at least three important areas: improvements in communications technology, developments in computer technology, and creation of a new scientific basis for education called performance technology.

References

Ashby, Eric. "Machines, Understandings and Learning: Reflection on Technology in Education." *The Graduate Journal* 7 no.2. Austin: The University of Texas, 1967.

Harless, J.H. Presentation to the Educational Technology Faculty. College of Education, The University of Georgia, Athens. 1986.

The Northwest Report : The Newsletter of the Northwest Regional Educational Laboratory. "Technology aids rural schools: Distance education shows great promise." (Jan 89):1,6.

The Technology Teacher. "High Tech News Column." 48 no.8(May-June 1989):32.

Suggested Readings

American School Board Journal, "The Electronic School." 175no.9 (September 1988): A1-A32.

Boyd, Gary. The Impact Of Society On Educational Technology. *British Journal of Educational Technology.* 19 no.2 (May 88): 114-22.

Gage, N.L. *The Scientific Basis of the Art of Teaching.* New York: Teachers College Press, 1978.

MacDaniels, Gary. Can Computers Improve the Thinking of Students in American Schools? in *Essays on the Intellect,* edited by Frances R. Link, 143-50. Washington: Association for Supervision and Curriculum Development, 1985.

Perelman, Lewis J. "Restructuring the System." *Phi Delta Kappan* 70 no.1 (Sep 88):20-24, 1988.

Saelter, Paul. *A History of Instructional Technology.* New York: McGraw-Hill, 1968.

Skinner, B. F. *The Technology of Teaching.* New York: Appleton-Century-Crofts, 1968.

Chapter 3
Technology As Product: Hardware Considerations

This chapter addresses the aspect of selection of hardware, with the emphasis on the hardware, itself, although the process of selection is mentioned. The reason for dedicating a separate chapter to hardware is because the alternatives are so diverse, extensive, and important. The purpose of this chapter is to describe several of the current hardware "systems" which are most suitable for educational applications. The chapter does not address "traditional technologies" such as projection equipment, television, or books. The chapter does describe contemporary technologies which are not commonly used today but have been shown to be useful, are available and ready to use. The technologies described in this chapter are microcomputers, interactive videotape and videodisc equipment, computer communications equipment, telecommunications systems, and voice generating systems.

Microcomputers

Microcomputers are described first because of the current popularity of this technology and also because they add so much capability to almost any school program. Microcomputers add a great deal to education as an administrative tool, an instructional support tool, a teaching tool, and as an object of instruction.

Microcomputers, like any other computer, consist of four essential components, one very important component, and several additional optional components. The essential components for any computer are:

_ The Central Processing Unit (CPU)
_ The Main Memory
_ The Input Device
_ The Output Device

The very important component is:

_The Mass Storage Device

Additional components, sometimes referred to as peripheral devices, which are available, and often nice to have , include:
_ Modem
_ Printer
_ Tablet
_ Mouse
_ Game Paddles
_ Platter

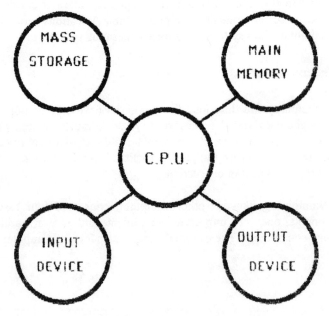

Illustration 3
Major Components of Any Computer System

_ Color Graphics Printer
_ A Hard Disk, and an Additional Disk Drive
_ A Voice Synthesizer (described later in this chapter)
_ Videodisc Player (described later in this chapter)

Essential Components

The essential components of any computer system include the central processing unit (CPU), memory, one input device and one output device. The essential components are the indispensable components; without any one of them, the product is not a computer. Furthermore, when comparing or selecting microcomputer hardware, these are the major components that must be compared and evaluated.

The capabilities of the essential components of the computer are largely dependent on the microchips which are installed. In fact, it is the "miracle of the microchip" which makes this, and other technologies,

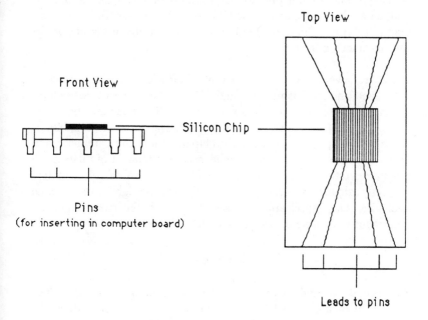

Illustration 4
Integrated Circuit

available today. The microchip is a product of efforts toward miniaturization in electronics.

Electronics depends upon circuits. Solid state electronics consists of circuits made up of electric-conducting metal strips adhered to boards called circuit boards. The first circuit boards were huge compared to the "chips" of today. Early computers were monstrous devices which consisted of panel after panel (as large as a wall) of wired electrical circuits. Even the circuit boards installed in television sets, radios, and later computers were so large that the "pocket sized" electronic devices of today were not possible. Only through development of printed circuits on silicon was miniaturization made possible.

Central Processing Unit

The central processing unit (CPU) is the "brain" of the computer. The CPU performs two major functions: 1) it controls all other components of the system through pre-stored programs or electrical circuits installed on microchips, and 2) the CPU performs arithmetic operations. It adds, subtracts, multiplies, and divides, also through programs or circuits installed on the CPU chip.

There are several CPU chips currently being installed in microcomputers and, though it is not essential to know the names of these chips, it is important to know the capabilities of the CPU when making a purchase. Two factors should be considered in evaluating the capabilities of the CPU chip: 1) the speed of the chip in performing arithmetic, and 2) the accuracy of the arithmetic in terms of the number of digits it will calculate to the right of the decimal point. Most microcomputers presently calculate accurately up to 16 digits to the right of the decimal point. For most applications, however, speed is the more important criteria for evaluating the microcomputers capability.

Memory

The second essential component of the microcomputer is memory. The amount of memory available determines, to a very great extent, the capability of the equipment. Memory also resides on microchips which are installed in the microcomputer. Memory is characterized in terms of the number of "bytes" of data which can be stored. Most microcomputers sold today have a minimum of 128,000 bytes of memory, or 128 kilobytes. Some microcomputers, come with as much as 1,000,000 bytes, or 1 megabyte, of memory.

A single byte of memory consists of a group of "bits." The word "bit" stands for "binary digit" which is a single digit (number) in the base two number system. The base two number system consists of the digits 0 and 1. A group of 0 and/or 1 digits together make up a byte. Some computers use bytes which consist of 8 bits, some use 16 bits per byte, and some use more, depending on the capability of the CPU. The size of the byte (8, 16, 32 bits or more) which can be "read" (processed) by the computer determines, in part, the speed of the computer's performance. Many recent microcomputers use 16 and 32 bit bytes, although most personal computers still use 8 bit bytes.

Input Device

An input device is the essential piece of equipment which is used to enter information into the computer's main memory for processing by the CPU. The most common input device used today is the standard keyboard. Virtually all microcomputers today come equipped with keyboards for typing information into the computer. Other types of input devices are available, and often desirable, but only one is essential.

Output Device

An output device is used to display or reveal the contents of portions of the computer's memory. The primary output device used today on most computers is the cathode-ray tube (sometimes called the CRT) which is the main component of computer monitors and television sets. Today's microcomputers come with either color or monochrome monitors. Color monitors are considerably more expensive than monochrome, about 3 times as much, and are not always necessary for educational applications, though they are often more aesthetically pleasing to use.

The next most commonly used output device is a printer. The CRT and printer are usually used together, but only one device is essential.

Very Important Component

Information storage, as well as easy access to the information, are very important considerations when using a computer. However, most computers lose the information held in memory when the device is turned off. There is, therefore, an important need for a device which will store information as long as required, but one which provides quick and easy accessibility, as well. The device which meets these requirements is a disk drive. Information is stored on a diskette which has been inserted into the disk drive. Disk drives use either 3.5, 5, or 8 inch diskettes, the most common being the 5 inch diskette.

A computer system "package" may be sold with one or two disk drives, but two are better. Having two disk drives offers several advantages, such as being able to copy files and disks.

Peripheral Devices

What has been described as essential and very important is all that is needed to assemble a basic microcomputer system that can be used in the home, in the office or work place, or in the school. The peripheral devices described below add convenience, aesthetics, and/or variety to the capability of a computer system.

Modem

The name "modem" is short for the term "modulate/demodulate." A modem is a device which makes possible communication between computer users at different locations, whether in different areas of the same building, or in distant locations, many miles apart. Information is transmitted over communication lines, usually telephone lines.

Printer

A printer is a device for producing paper copies, or "hard copies", of information that is stored in the computer's memory. Most users of microcomputers find printers indispensable, especially for management types of applications. Printers come in basic models: dot matrix printers and letter-quality printers. Dot matrix printers form the printed characters with a combination of many small dots which can be discerned in some cases. Letter quality printers form characters by impression of the type font against the carbon, in much the same way as typewriters do. Dot matrix printers are less expensive, permit the printing of graphic images, and generally produce what is called "near letter quality" print. Letter quality printers, on the other hand, produce copies which are indistinguishable from high quality typewriters, and consequently can produce limited graphics.

Graphics Tablet

A graphics tablet is a pad on which pictures can be drawn with a digitizing "pen." The image is created "on-screen" in the computer's memory. The pictures produced can be saved on disk and/or printed on a dot matrix printer.

Mouse

A mouse is a small box that sets on the desktop, connected to the computer by an electrical cord. A "mouse" is used instead of the keyboard

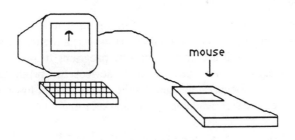

Illustration 5
A Mouse

to perform many operations of the computer. It is convenient for producing pictures and performing operations such as loading and saving files, selecting applications, and for interacting with the computer operating system. Moving the mouse on the desktop plane causes corresponding moves of a pointer pictograph on the screen for making selections or lines, shapes, etc., for drawing pictures.

Games Paddles

Games paddles are small devices, about the same size as the mouse, convenient to fit in the hand. Games paddles come in pairs for use by one or two persons. They have knobs, which, when rotated, move a pointer (or whatever design character is used) around on the screen of the CRT. The games paddles also contain a push button to trigger other actions on the screen, such as swinging a bat or pushing an object. Games paddles are mostly used for games, as the name suggests, but they can also be used in computer system applications which require considerable external input, such as raising or lowering sounds on a musical scale. "Joy sticks" have similar capability, and operate in a similar way except for the use of a separate lever controlling dial axis movement.

Plotter

A plotter is similar to a dot matrix printer in that it marks dots on paper to form characters and symbols. However, a plotter uses pens of various colors which are coordinated by programs to produce multi-colored images. Plotters are excellent devices for producing color graphics but are being challenged by the emergence of low cost, high-quality, color printers available on the market today.

Color Graphics Printer

Dot matrix printers are now available which employ one of two techniques for producing color graphics copy. One technique uses several different colored ribbons which are substituted as required during the printing process. The other technique uses a single multi-colored ribbon. The quality of the color produced by either of these techniques is outstanding.

Additional Disk Drives

Additional disk drives greatly enhance the computer's capability. Two disk drives make it easy to create backup copies and to copy files from one disk to another, or to copy entire diskettes without complications and anxiety.

Voice Synthesis

Voice synthesis is a method of producing near-human quality voice on digital computer disks. This equipment is more thoroughly discussed later in the chapter, but it should be noted at this time that the equipment needed is relatively inexpensive when viewed in terms of the added quality it may provide in instructional programs on computers. The prospects are especially exciting with regard to mentally handicapped individuals, poor readers and problem readers.

Videodisc

Videodisc is also described more thoroughly in a separate section of this chapter. Videodisc is mentioned here because it can be used as a peripheral mass storage device for a computer system. Videodiscs are similar to videotape in that they can store video and audio data which can be displayed on a CRT as still pictures or motion pictures. With appropriate interfaces connected, some computer systems can display both images for videodisc and computer data, simultaneously.

Interactive Video

Interactive video involves the use of videotape or, preferably, videodisc players which provide a combination of still pictures, motion pictures, audio, and text on a standard screen. What makes these video displays *interactive* is the capability of addressing locations on the tape or disc from within a computer program which are designed to respond to input from the user of the computer. A very simple illustration of this would be to provide a sequence showing two chemicals violently reacting to one another anytime a student selects a chemical combination which would produce that result.

The use of videodisc rather than tape has some major advantages. Videodiscs can store as many as 54,000 single images on a single side. This means that many instructional programs might be designed so that a single disc would contain all necessary displays and changing discs would not be necessary. Second, because videodiscs are read by low power laser light, the access time to the beginning of any display from the disc is almost instantaneous. A third advantage of disc over tape is that they are extremely durable and not easily harmed by handling.

The initial cost of videodiscs and equipment is not very high, generally under $1,000. However, making your own disc is very expensive and there are very few discs available which are appropriate for educational applications. The process of producing an educational videodisc requires high quality design of the necessary screen displays, artistic production of the needed visuals or action, professional production of a film or videotape, and conversion of videodisc. All in all, until publishers begin to produce such products, the only available applications will be those produced in research and development laboratories in colleges and universities. However, where interactive video applications may serve a special educational purpose such as teaching medicine or dentistry, foreign languages, and some handicapped areas, the effort to produce, at least, interactive videotapes might be well worth the price in learner outcomes.

Computer Communications Equipment

The primary piece of equipment to add communications capability to a computer is the modem, already described in this chapter. The other necessary components are basically software packages which will be discussed in the next chapter. For the time being, and assuming the existence of at least two modems, one on each end of the communications link, two basic approaches to computer communications will be mentioned.

First is the establishment and use of computer bulletin boards. These are called bulletin boards because they function like bulletin boards in that individuals can post messages for others to read at their convenience. To establish a bulletin board requires only a software package on a designated computer with a modem for receiving calls, modems at the other end of the link - in the classroom or lounge, etc. — and telephones at both ends. The total cost for equipment is well justified in terms of communications capability within the reach of a bulletin board. This capability also adds the capability of joining large scale bulletin board systems and accessing national services offering large information data bases.

The second approach for using communications capability is for real time interaction between two or more computer systems, sometimes called computer conferencing. This usually involves the use of modems and telephone lines, but also requires a larger computer which has greater time sharing capability in order to support at least two computers simultaneously.

Telecommunications Systems

Telecommunications system refers to the use of telephone communications as with standard home and office telephones and computer networking as described above. These are not new or remarkable uses of telecommunications and little information about them seems necessary. What is relatively new and unique about modem telecommunications is the use of satellites and radio signals to transmit and receive information. The use of satellites is far more cost effective than telephone cables, can cover large geographical areas, can transmit many channels simultaneously, and can circumvent geographical obstacles such as mountains and oceans easily. Private businesses such as the major television networks, already make extensive use of satellite communications and they will soon be more readily available for public use.

Use of this system of communication to receive programs is already quite popular in rural areas which are today dotted with satellite dishes for receiving over 100 television channels. Cost for such service is quite reasonable but problems still remain over legal issues pertaining to accessing and using channels which are privately owned and operated. These issues are being addressed very seriously at the present time.

Capability to make telecommunications interactive requires that the sender also have transmission facilities which are considerably more expensive than receiving dishes. However, regional systems which can be shared should make the cost of such capability non-prohibitive.

Voice Capabilities

Audio capability with computers is available, at modest cost, for both voice input and synthesized or digitized voice output. Of all the peripherals available, voice systems may add more quality to computer applications than any other device at similar prices. This may be the most appropriate capability to add to computer systems purchased for instructional purposes. In fact, voice synthesis with a system having a color monitor provides the potential for delivering some of the best instruction available anywhere at any cost depending, of course, on the quality of the courseware design.

Voice input systems usually operate with an added circuit board and a microphone. The user builds a vocabulary of words or phrases from the keyboard onto the screen. After the vocabulary is specified and that part of the session ended, the computer introduces each word or phrase on the screen and instructs the user to speak the word or phrase into the microphone. Each word or phrase then has a voice pattern associated with it. From then on, when the voice pattern is spoken again, the associated word or phrase is assumed by the computer. The voice patterns can also be viewed on the screen displayed as graphic sound wave patterns.

Voice output is provided either by voice synthesizers or by voice devices. Early systems simply took sound wave patterns and converted them to digits which drove mechanically produced sounds in a voice box. The method produced very poor quality sound and used considerable memory. The next generation of voice synthesis used phonemes rather than words but worked in a similar way. However, the digitized phonemes, when combined into words produced outstanding quality voice. Unfortunately, the average system required a full 64 K of memory for one minute of speech, making it quite unfeasible for instructional use. Now, however, for a relatively modest cost, a voice synthesis system is available which provides greater flexibility in the application of voice synthesis, high quality voice, and uses little or no random access memory.

Interactive Videotape and Videodisc

Interactive video, when controlled by microcomputers, is one of the most powerful and exciting marriages of two educational technologies. What interactive video provides is outstanding quality, high resolution video screens for display in instructional programs. Videotape and videodisc are quite similar in the displays which can be produced but videodisc provides faster access and greater storage capability.

Videotape and videodisc operate on similar principles. Both media store photographically reproduced displays which can be controlled either manually or by commands in a computer program. The control of these devices involves turning the device on or off and selecting portions of the medium to be displayed as a moving or still display.

Producing original videotapes to accompany computer-based instructional programs simply requires a videotape camera and recording device. This is also the first step in producing an original videodisc which is a videotape reproduced by laser on a shiny disc. Commercially produced tapes and discs are also available at very reasonable prices, though seldom coordinated with computer-based instructional programs.

The advantage of interactive videotape is the lower cost. Disadvantages include the slowness of accessing a particular segment of the tape and the consequent damage resulting from the wear and tear of searching the tape. The advantages of videodisc include a two second, or less, access time of any frame on the disc (54,000 individual frames per side), and the durability of the disc, itself. In fact, some proponents maintain that when not in use as an instructional tool it can substitute as a frisbee. The disadvantage of videodisc is the cost of producing the final disc. However, this cost is rapidly being reduced and commercially produced discs can be acquired for as little as twelve dollars.

The potential of interactive video is rapidly being recognized as providing for some of the best instruction ever known for a reasonable investment in time and money.

Summary

This chapter focuses on technological products which are essentially hardware and which have considerable potential in educational improvement. The description provided for various hardware should be used as a basis for identifying appropriate technology to meet educational needs and to solve educational problems. Of course, hardware is only one element of the improvement process and other considerations must take place at the same time. A familiarity with the hardware described is necessary as an early step in the process of planning, developing, implementing, and evaluating educational systems, including the selection of hardware as part of the process.

Suggested Readings

Chambers, Jack A. and Sprecher, Jerry A. *Computer-Assisted Instruction*. Englewood Cliffs: Prentice-Hall, 1983.

Conniffe, Patricia. *Computer Dictionary*. New York: Scholastic Press, 1984.

Dence, Jean. "Interactive Videodiscs: A New Instructional Technology." *Business Education Forum* 42no.6(March 1988):3-5.

D'Ignazio, Fred. "Bringing the 1990's to the Classroom of Today." *Phi Delta Kappan* v. 70, no. 1, (Sept. 1988).

Knirk, Frederick G. and Gustafson, Kent L. *Instructional Technology*. New York: Holt, Rinehart and Winston, 1986.

Ley, Kathryn L. "CD ROM: Searching with Speed." *Media and Methods* March/April 1989.

Reynolds, Karen. "Videodisks Serve Up Learning Opportunities on a Silver Platter." *The American School Board Journal* v. 175, no. 3, March 1988.

Trainor, Timothy N. *Computer Literacy Concepts and Applications*. Santa Cruz, CA: Mitchell Publishing, Inc., 1984.

Chapter 4
Technology as Product:
Software Considerations

Technology does not thrive on hardware, alone. Hardware often gets all the glory but, behind the scenes, there is software which determines how, when, where, and why the hardware does what it does! Software is the term applied to the "instructions," commands, directions, and programs that make hardware perform their operations. Well designed software is, beyond a doubt, absolutely essential for effective technology. High quality software may not even be dependent on hardware, as hardware is dependent upon software. When software is designed to solve a problem, the hardware to be used is sometimes a secondary consideration, for which the well designed software can be adapted. Sometimes, software alone - without any obvious hardware - can solve problems.

Several types of software are discussed in this chapter. The discussion is confined, for the most part, to existing software for educational use until later in the chapter. The early part of the chapter discusses software for instructional use, for instructional support use, for administrative use, and for personal use. Later in the chapter, the creation of original applications through the use of programming languages, authoring systems, and expert systems is discussed.

Software

Software is so called because it represents ideas, thoughts, and instructions, as opposed to equipment, about how to solve a problem. Early software for electronic devices consisted of the plan, or design, of electronic circuits to perform a series of functions. These plans were converted into electronic circuits which were placed on circuit boards and installed in appropriate equipment. The software is the plan, design, or set of instructions for using technology. A written recipe is software which is designed to facilitate the use of equipment and ingredients to produce edible meals. A drawing of a house plan is software for constructing a house. A landscape design is a plan for producing well landscaped grounds. Written music is the software for making musical productions.

Using technology requires that instructions be given to the hardware and operating software to make the system perform unique functions. For example, to retrieve an application from disk to memory, the command "load [filename]" is often used. In a BASIC program, the statement, "print" followed by text in quotes will cause the computer to display whatever is enclosed in quotes on the display device. Commands and/or statements such as print, write, goto, load, save, run, if...then, and gosub are special words which make up a language for communicating with computers. Computer languages and programming languages are ways in which a user communicates directly with a computer to make it function appropriately.

Many applications are available which allow the user to communicate their instructions in a very normal language. These applications usually prompt the user to enter information and/or data for that particular use. These kinds of applications are addressed next in this chapter.

Applications Software

Applications software is available for almost any conceivable use that can be addressed by technology. This chapter discusses software applications that address direct instruction, instructional support, and administrative support. In each of these areas, however, there should be made one distinction among software packages: those that are generic packages and can be applied to each of the areas, and those that are special purpose applications designed especially for each of the areas.

Instructional Software

Generic software that can be used for instructional purposes is, perhaps, best represented by word processing packages. These can be easily adapted as direct instructional tools for teaching keyboard skills, composition, reading and writing. Other generic software packages that should be available in schools for instructional purposes might include spread sheets, data base packages, and statistics packages, though their applicability for direct instruction has not been clearly established except in business curricula. Various graphics packages, of course, have considerable use in art curriculum.

Special purpose applications for direct instruction include drill and practice lessons, tutorials, simulations, and problem solving programs in virtually every curriculum area taught in schools. Quality, of course, varies tremendously and careful review and evaluation is necessary to acquire high quality applications. Rather than listing curriculum areas or, worse, specific applications to instruction, a list of suppliers of such software appears in Part III of this book.

Software which includes voice output is also available, on a limited basis, in many curricular areas. Applications of this kind of software must be located through publishers' advertisements. Likewise, there are some suppliers of videodisc software. These kinds of applications can best be discovered through the diligent searching of publishers advertisements and word-of-mouth among interested and involved individuals and groups.

Instructional Support Software

Several uses can be made of generic software for instructional support. Spread sheets can be readily adapted to keeping various classroom records, including grades, and providing automatic calculations and production of reports. Data base applications are very useful for maintaining students' permanent records over long periods and for producing legal reports such as attendance, grades, and discipline records. Data base systems can be adapted to producing tests and maintaining records on test performance. With the use of optical scanning equipment which is interfaced with a data base system, much of the clerical work of teachers can be significantly reduced. Word processing software may also be an instructional support tool when communication of information is an important part of a task. Word processing packages, like graphics packages, can be extremely useful for producing specialized instructional materials.

The use of generic word processing and graphics software for producing instructional materials should be emphasized a bit more. Handouts, overhead projections, and displays can be produced easily with word and graphic processing programs on most microcomputers. The quality of these materials is nearly equivalent to that of commercially produced materials today. With the use of color printers which are now available, the quality may exceed anything available commercially due to its local relevance to the community, school, or even individual students. Teachers can use these systems to great advantage for communicating with parents, for example.

Special purpose software for instructional support is also readily available on most microcomputers for most applications. There are dedicated test generating systems, test scoring systems, grade recording systems, grade reporting systems, attendance keeping systems, and systems for producing specific instructional materials such as crossword puzzles and word find games.

Administrative Software

Most generic software packages were designed for typical administrative functions. Therefore, the use of spread sheet applications, data base applications, word processing, and statistical packages are quite adaptable to the school situation. These generic packages can effectively and efficiently maintain all kinds of records, budgets, accounting ledgers, school attendance, inventories, staff, and activities. Most school administrative applications are sufficiently large that the generic systems, often designed for specific hardware, are the most likely source of support.

Certain school administrative functions require special purpose packages also. Specifically, the functions of scheduling students, staff, and facilities, the maintenance of approved lunchroom facilities and service, keeping average daily attendance (ADA) records for legal reporting may require specially and locally produced software. These can be acquired commercially but, due to some statewide needs for uniformity, many states produce their own special purpose software for administrative services.

Programming Software

The need for programming capability within schools is two-fold. First, many schools will want to at least alter some of the available software to fit local needs and, possibly, to produce some original software specifically for local needs. This approach offers some advantage over trying to purchase everything ready made in that it offers the opportunity to tailor-make some applications, especially for instructional and instructional support purposes. Second, there will continue to be pressures on schools to teach programming skills to students at all grade levels, and even to adults. These two reasons, alone, will likely justify having available several programming languages.

Programming as an Aid to Instruction

Most educational applications today are written in either BASIC (Beginners All-purpose Symbolic Instruction Code), PASCAL, or PILOT. Also, most people who learn one of these languages can usually learn the others rather quickly. There already exists so much software for educational use that is written in these languages, that someone will be needed to improve and repair existing applications. However, applications packages called authoring systems are rapidly becoming available which may, one day, take the place of programming languages as tools for creating educational software. For the present, BASIC, PASCAL, and PILOT are useful for both fixing existing software and for creating original software applications.

Authoring systems are rapidly becoming available, therefore making it possible to avoid learning traditional programming just for the purpose of producing educational applications of computers. For large numbers of teachers, authoring systems will offer the ability for them to produce educational software without much training in computers. Teachers, then, can be *designers* of software and let the authoring systems do the actual programming. Several prominent authoring systems are listed in Part III of this book.

Programming as an Object of Instruction

More will be said about teaching about technology in chapter 5. For now, it may be important to note the present demand being felt in schools to teach programming as a technical skill. Programming may someday be replaced by sophisticated expert systems such as authoring systems, described above. These systems, indeed, require little formal programming skill. However, programming - taught well - seems to foster the development of what might appropriately be called *algorithmic thinking*. Algorithmic thinking refers to the ability to envision and describe a systematic solution to a problem. Experience, and some limited research, tends to show that computer programming requires that kind of thinking and that one result of learning programming is to improve or increase algorithmic thinking. This kind of problem solving has long been, and likely will continue to be, a major goal of education and will, hence, continue to make the teaching of programming a desirable feature of schooling.

Algorithmic Thinking and Programming

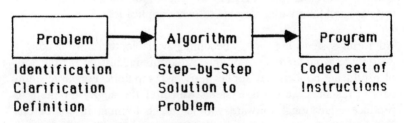

Illustration 6
Teaching Programming and Algorithmic Thinking

Software for Programming Interactive Video

Coordinating the display of video at specified points in a computer-based instructional program requires only that appropriate commands appear in the computer program at appropriate locations. The specific commands used depend upon the brand or model of the equipment used and, in some cases, on the software used. For example, on the APPLE microcomputer, the command word to be used is the character "V" followed by numerals or other codes which specify the location for the playback machine to begin and end its display of prerecorded pictorials.

Summary

The importance of software for directing hardware operations is stressed in this chapter. The term "software" is described and briefly discussed as to its meaning. Several relevant applications of software are presented in the areas of instructional software, instructional support software, and administrative software discerning, where appropriate, between generic software packages and special purpose applications. Finally, two aspects of programming software are presented, first for aiding in the altering or creating of educational software and, second, as an object of instruction.

Suggested Readings

Freyd, Pamela. "What Educators Really Want in Software Design." *Media and Methods* (March-April 1989):44-47.

Harte, David V. "The Search for 21st Century Mindware." *Community, Technical and Junior College Journal* 58no.2(Oct-Nov 1987):50-53.

Lechner, H. D. *The Computer Chronicles.* Belmont, CA.: Wadsworth Publishing Company, 1984.

McKeown, Patrick G. *Living with Computers.* San Diego: Harcourt Brace Jovanovich, Publishers, 1986.

Olivas, Jerry. "Yes, You Can Run the Front Office on a Microcomputer System." *Classroom Computer Learning* 8no.6(March 1989): 46-49.

Rosen, Marion. "LEGO Meets LOGO." *Classroom Computer Learning*, 8no.7(April 1988):50-51, 54, 56-58.

Widerquist, Kristine. "Course Design for Training Secondary Teachers to Develop Interactive Videodisc Courseware." *Technological Horizons in Education* 14no.6, (Feb 1987):68-72.

Chapter 5
Teaching About Technology

Teaching programming for a variety of purposes was briefly mentioned in Chapter 4. This chapter will address the need to incorporate the subject of technology in the curricula at all levels of education.

The purpose for including any subject in the curriculum is to provide opportunities for learners to acquire skills and knowledge for becoming fully functioning humans. Today's society has become so technologically oriented that these skills and knowledge are almost imperative for successful adulthood. Today's workers are surrounded by technology in the workplace, the home, and in every area of commerce. To avoid teaching about technology would be as serious as if the teaching of reading and writing were avoided. Teaching about technology is no longer just desirable, it is essential for personal problem solving and for vocational success later in life.

This chapter discusses the content which should be taught, and the levels at which it could be taught. It is hoped that all schools will find ways to incorporate technology in their curricula, both as a personal tool and as a problem solving tool in every subject area. Teachers will need the skills and knowledge of technology not only for education, but also for use in personal life, as well as in the subject areas being taught.

Skills and Knowledge Continuum

Educators need to possess the same skills and knowledge as do most people to live in this technological world, but they need to know more. Educators need to know the subject well enough to teach it to others, and the curriculum must teach how to learn information and skills efficiently (Lesgold, 1986). For this reason, a careful analysis of what should be taught is necessary. Following is a brief summary of what many writers and experts think should be taught to most, if not all, people.

First to be considered are the topics which should be included in the curriculum. A general pattern of agreement has emerged that the following broad topics should be considered in any computer curriculum:

1. Hardware literacy
2. Software literacy
3. Programming literacy
4. Social Impact literacy

Next, to be considered is the question of when to teach these topics and to what depth at each level. There seems to be a need to learn about technology which can conveniently be divided into four levels:

1. Awareness
2. Utilization
3. Production
4. Specialization

Number of People Affected

Many..Few

    Awareness   Utilization   Production   Specialization

Low...High

Level of Skill and Knowledge Required

Illustration 7
Skills and Knowledge Continuum

The continuum in Illustration 7 shows that awareness is the lowest level of content which should be offered at any level and which should be acquired by almost everybody in America today. Specialization, on the other hand, refers to highly complex skills and knowledge which probably need only be learned by those specializing in research, development, or teaching about computer science, a relatively few professionals. Utilization refers to those skills and knowledge which are needed to use existing applications, which will involve a great many people, but most likely will increase even more each year. Production skills and knowledge is for those who will earn at least part of their earnings directly from the technology business and industries.

	Awareness	Utilization	Production	Specialization
Hardware	K-3	K-3		
	4-5	4-5	4-5	
				6-8
			9-12	9-12
				13
Software	K-3	K-3		
	4-5	4-5	4-5	
			6-8	
			9-12	9-12
				13
Programming	K-3	K-3	K-3	
		4-5	4-5	
			6-8	
				9-12
				13
Social impact	K-3			
	4-5			
	6-8			
	9-12			

Illustration 8
Placement of Computer Topics in Curriculum

Educators will need to determine, while planning their curricula, the grades in which these topics should be introduced. The distribution of these topics, as well as the level of difficulty or complexity at which they are taught, will vary from state to state and from school district to school district, at least. Whatever decisions are made at the local school level, the following distribution might be carefully considered as one way of organizing the curriculum.

Educators planning curricula will also have to determine the *specific* skills and knowledge under each topic and for each grade level at which the topics are to be presented. This step in planning curriculum has traditionally been the responsibility of state departments of education or local schools. Therefore, only illustrative statements will be presented here for each level and for each topic. Those involved in planning curriculum will need to spell out more objectives for their specific school system and schools.

Hardware Skills and Knowledge

What hardware skills and knowledge should be taught at what level from the continuum offered in this chapter? Note that this does not address the question of grade level squarely, but may suggest appropriate grade placement of skills and knowledge. A summary table of illustrative sub-topics might include:

	K - 3	4 - 5	6 - 8	9 - 12
Awareness		Microcomputers Basic Principals	Components	History
Utilization	Keyboarding		Advanced Use	Mastery
Production			How Produced	Type of hardware
Specialization				Architecture

Translating these sub-topics into statements of skill and knowledge then needs to be accomplished for each of the grade levels specified.

Using the above list, the requisite skills and knowledge would include the following.

Kindergarten Through Third Grades

Awareness
1. To distinguish a microcomputer by its major components, which are plainly visible, from other electronic devices.

Utilization
1. To perform traditional touch typing techniques on a computer keyboard using known words with no speed requirements.

Fourth Through Fifth Grades

Awareness
1. To name the necessary major components of a computer system.

Utilization
1. To use keyboard functions to perform the operations of loading, running, saving, locking, and unlocking files.

Sixth Through Eighth Grades

Awareness
1. To describe five historical precedents to the development of today's microcomputers.

Utilization
1. To copy files and diskettes using system operations and/or utility programs.

Production
1.To describe the process for producing the microchip on silicon using reduction techniques.

Ninth Through Twelfth Grades

Awareness
1. To describe the basic principles of computer operations including the use of the binary number system and electronic circuitry.

Utilization
1. To determine adequate equipment requirements for a given set of specifications for an operational system.

Production
1. To identify three levels (sizes) of computers by the attributes of function, and capability.

Specialization
1. To thoroughly describe the functions and operations of a given computer system.

Software Skills and Knowledge

Skills and knowledge pertaining to software should address the evaluation and use of existing software and the creation of original software for solving unique problems. There is no age or grade level which has been determined to be the best for beginning to learn about software. Therefore, the grade placement of various topics, again, must be left to the state or local schools. However, an example of how these skills and knowledge might be distributed is shown below.

	K-3	4-5	6-8	9-12
Awareness	Applications	Packages	Integrated packages	Design Features
Utilization	C.A.I.	W.P., D.B.	All software	Comparative
Production		Reports	Projects	Evaluation
Specialization				Redesign

Broken down by grade levels, and restated as performance, these subtopics would include:

Kindergarten Through Third Grades

Awareness
1. To identify by functional use the names of three applications of computers in their lives.

Utilization
1. To use computer-assisted instruction programs successfully without technical help.

Fourth Through Fifth Grades

Awareness
1. To identify four types of application packages available commercially.

Utilization
1. To use word processing, data base, and spread sheet packages.

Production
1. To use a data base or spread sheet package to produce a report.

Sixth Through Eighth Grades

Awareness
1. To describe the meaning of "Integrated software."

Utilization
1. To use any software package successfully without any technical assistance.

Production
1. To conduct a project which solves a problem with any applications package.

Ninth Through Twelfth Grades

Awareness
1. To explain the advantages of integrated software.

Utilization
1. To select and successfully use an application package for the first time.

Production
1. To evaluate software applications based on predetermined criteria.

Specialization
1. To identify strengths and weakness in a given software package.

Programming Skills and Knowledge

Programming skills and knowledge go beyond merely learning a computer programming language. (Individuals who can only code programs in a language such as BASIC or PASCAL are not really programming, they are merely codifying instructions given them by someone else.) Programming has come to be thought of as a three phase process: defining the problem, creating the step-by-step solution (often called the algorithm), and coding the steps as instructions to the equipment to be used. When teaching programming, the most important concept to be taught is what is becoming known as "algorithmic thinking." That is, learners acquire the skills and knowledge required for all three phases. Such skills and knowledge might be distributed over the years of schooling as follows.

	K - 3	4 - 5	6 - 8	9 - 12
Awareness	Logic	Linear Logic	Structured Logic	Complex Logic
Utilization	Problems	Problems	Problems	Design
Production	LOGO	BASIC	PASCAL	Expert Systems
Specialization			Design	Art. Intel.

Again, these need to be further broken down into more specific statements of required performance to master the skills and knowledge required. That might appear as follows.

Kindergarten Through Third Grades

Awareness
1. To recognize reasonable IF ... THEN propositions such as
[IF] it is night [THEN] daytime will follow.

Utilization
1. To determine the solution to the problem, "If it is below 32
degrees outside, what should you wear?"

Production
1. To draw pictures using simple Turtle Graphics commands
in LOGO.

Fourth Through Fifth Grades

Awareness
1. To identify simple problems which can be solved with linear
logic.

Utilization
1. To solve a simple program with linear logic.

Production
1. To develop a simple program in BASIC.

Sixth Through Eighth Grades

Awareness
1. To distinguish between structured and linear programming.

Utilization
1. To design a problem solution using structured logic.

Production
1. To develop a structured program using PASCAL to solve a
given problem.

Specialization
1. To design a structured solution to a generic problem such as processing words.

Ninth Through Twelfth Grades

Awareness
1. To identify problems that are appropriate for different types of logical solution.

Utilization
1. To develop a solution for a generic problem such as word processing or record keeping.

Production
1. To develop a PASCAL program for a generic problem such as word processing.

Specialization
1. To recognize problems which can be solved by artificial intelligence applications.

Social Impact

Most people have acknowledged the impact which technology has had on their lives, although perhaps not consciously. Even an idle expression such as , "I don't know what he would do without Monday Night Football," is an acknowledgment of the impact of television. But, more importantly, a recognition of ways in which technology affects the economy, the marketplace, transportation, leisure time, and a myriad of other aspects of human life, is important for a responsible citizenry. Some of the relevant understandings could be presented at various grade levels as follows.

	K - 3	4 - 5	6 - 8	9 - 12
Awareness	Contrast History	Transportation	Government	Ethics

If these were defined more specifically and in terms of performance at the various grade levels, they might look like the following.

Kindergarten Through Third Grades
    1. To identify differences between the lives of children today and of fifty years ago.

Fourth Through Fifth Grade
    1. To identify the difference between mechanical and electronic operations and functions.

Sixth Through Eighth Grades
    1. To describe the effects of technology on democratic elections over the past 25 years.

Ninth Through Twelfth Grades
    1. To define the ethical issues of copying protected software.

Summary

This chapter focuses on the need to include skills and knowledge for dealing with technology in the curriculum. Pressures from the public as well as common sense suggest that today's students need to learn to use technology for successful adulthood. This need can only be viewed as growing greater each year.

The chapter addresses four major topics which include hardware, software, programming, and social impact of technology and which should probably be included in the curriculum at all levels of education. It also suggests a continuum of skills and knowledge which begins with awareness of technology, to utilization of technology, to production of technology, to specialization for technology. The chapter stresses that states and local school agencies should be responsible for direct placement of these subjects in the curriculum.

References

Eisele, James E. "Computers: What Every Educator Really Ought'a Know." *Educational Technology* 23No.10(October, 1983):35.

Lesgold, Alan M. "Preparing Children for a Computer-Rich World." *Educational Leadership* 43no.6 March 1986:7-11.

Suggested Readings

Judd, Dorothy H. and Judd, Robert C. *Mastering the Micro*. Dallas: Scott, Foresman and Company, 1984.

Schall, William E., Leake, Lowell, Jr. and Whitaker, Donald R. *Computer Education: Literacy and Beyond*. Monterey: Brooks, Cole Publishing Company, 1986.

Sullivan, David R., Lewis, Theodore G. and Cook, Curtis R. *Computing Today*. Boston: Houghton Mifflin Company, 1985.

Vockell, Edward L. and Vockell, R. H. *Instructional Computing for Today's Teachers*. New York: Macmillan Publishing Company, 1984.

Chapter 6
Technology as Process:
Managing Implementation

Technology uses, or consists of, both hardware and software. But, technology also depends greatly upon people. People must create technology and they must use technology. This chapter is about how to use technology in an educational environment. Using technology effectively requires a systematic approach to the management of that technology. That is what is meant by the title of this chapter: technology as process is the systems approach to managing the technology to be implemented.

The only real requirement imposed by technology is that its use be systematic. Imagine, if you will, a television network operating without schedules, deadlines, rehearsals, and precise planning! Or, think of what happens to an automobile if maintenance is not routine and regular. CHAOS! Technology needs to be managed systematically or, in the popular vernacular, it may run amok.

There is no single systematic method of managing technology. However, there are characteristics that are present when the effort is systematic. These characteristics are that it is orderly, consistent, based upon established knowledge, and is replicable.

The plan presented in this chapter is offered as only one alternative. However, the plan possesses the characteristics described above and it is general enough to allow flexibility while being specific enough to permit successful utilization. The steps presented in the plan include:

1. Establishing Goals
2. Determining Needs
3. Setting Objectives
4. Developing the Solution
5. Managing the Implementation
6. Evaluating the Implementation

Establishing Goals

The very first thing that needs to be done during the planning process is to be certain that the goals are clear. This may be accomplished by an individual, by a small group, or by a large group. In business, industry, the military, and with many religious groups, the goals are predetermined by a small body, sometimes just by a single individual. However, experience has shown rather vividly that if people are expected to accept change willingly, they should be involved in the process of planning that change, and that may include the first step: establishing the objectives.

In education, the goals are usually established through careful consideration of the institution of schooling, itself, and the needs of the learners, and others involved in the educational process, including the community.

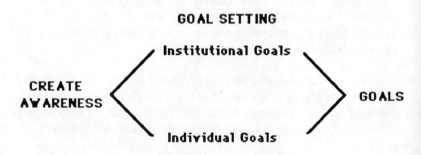

Illustration 9
Considerations in Establishing Goals

The first step in determining goals is to create an awareness of what the existing goals are. Seldom is it the case when goals are created for the first time. If there does not exist a current statement of goals, then one should be created. However, even in that event, there should be some evidence of intended goals. Normally, it is a matter of uncovering those goals, explicit or inferred. The goals which most need to be highlighted are those of the institution for the simple reason that they probably reflect those of the learners and the community around them. If they do reflect these constituents' interest, then those goal statements are sufficient. If they do not, goals should be written that reflect the concerns of these groups.

Determining Needs

Needs can be defined as unmet goals, provided those goals are important ones to all concerned. The unmet goals will be either those of the institution, the individuals involved, or the community or environment surrounding the community.

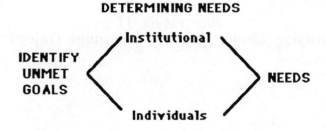

Illustration 10
Identifying Unmet Goals

Identifying unmet goals can be either through the use of quantitative or qualitative analysis, or both, as long as the data to be used is systematically and reliably gathered and analyzed. A reasonable combination, which usually produces valid results, is to survey all interested individuals and groups as to their opinions of whether or not the stated goals are being met.

Setting Objectives

To set the objectives for the plan to use technology, the needs which were identified must be analyzed for their type. Needs are based not only on unmet goals, but also are either the result of a lack of skills or knowledge, inadequate motivation, or deficiencies in the environment (Harless).

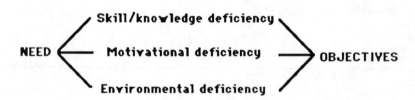

SETTING OBJECTIVES

NEED / Skill/knowledge deficiency / Motivational deficiency / Environmental deficiency → OBJECTIVES

Illustration 11
Identifying Unmet Needs to Determine Objectives

Each of the needs identified - the need for skills or knowledge, the need to improve the motivation or incentive system, or the need to improve the environment - must be addressed by specific performance objectives. These performance objectives should specify exactly what changes are to be brought about through the use of technology to meet the needs.

There are different approaches advocated for specifying objectives, and any of them could be effectively used (Tyler 1949, Mager 1962, Gagne 1974, Harless 1975). Whichever approach is adopted, the essence of objectives for planning change is that they tell:

1. WHO?

2. IS TO DO WHAT?

3. WHEN?

4. HOW?

And, that the objectives are clear and unambiguous.

Developing Solutions

With the objectives clearly stated, the next step is to plan the actual modification, change, or intervention which is to be introduced to attain those objectives. This step consists of two major components: specifying measurable criteria against which the success of the implementation can be evaluated, and defining step-by-step procedures for meeting the objectives.

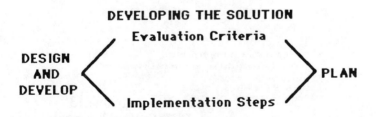

DEVELOPING THE SOLUTION

Evaluation Criteria

DESIGN AND DEVELOP

PLAN

Implementation Steps

Illustration 12
Developing the Solution Plan

The first part of this step may already be partially completed if the technology supported curriculum objectives stated are performance statements and if they answer the question, "Who does what, when, and how?" These statements will establish the criteria for evaluating effectiveness. If the objectives are not so stated, then criteria for success must be specified at this point. After the criteria are specified, instruments should be developed to be used for evaluating progress along the way to implementation and at the conclusion of major phases of the implementation.

The next part of this step is to lay out a specific plan of action. Again, if the objectives answer the question stated in the previous paragraph, a major part of the plan is predetermined and/or specified. The steps for implementation also specify who does what, when, and how as well as where and with what resources? An enormous help in creating this implementation plan is to use charts which specify events, activities, and time lines for identifying and accomplishing each step. An example of a modified PERT (Program Evaluation and Review Technique) type chart is shown below.

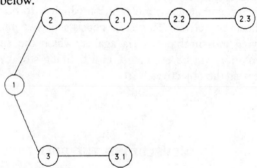

1. Start project.
2   Start specifications for tutorial system.
2 1 Complete study and analysis of hardware and software needs
2 2 Start bid writing
2 3 Send out bid requests.
2 4 Receive bid proposals

Illustration 13
PERT "type" Chart

In this diagram the implementation is scheduled to begin, Event #1, in April. The activities leading up to Event #2 are conducted during the month and the awareness activities are begun in May. Three sub-events, #2, #3, and #4 are conducted simultaneously to be concluded by the beginning of the month of June. This is a very brief example, but

one which illustrates how such a diagrammatic scheme can help guide
the implementation steps.

Implementation

The solution is planned, step-by-step. This is what is known as an algorithm - a step-by-step solution to a problem. Though the steps to solution are known, the technology to be used has yet to be decided upon.
The first decision that must be made is to select appropriate software
that addresses the problem. The second step is to select hardware.
The third step is to develop the participants' skills and knowledge to
implement the solution.

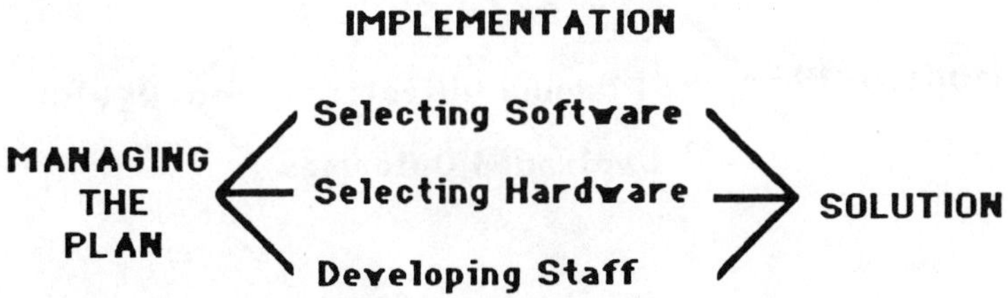

IMPLEMENTATION

**MANAGING
THE
PLAN**   ⟨ Selecting Software
   ← Selecting Hardware   → **SOLUTION**
   Developing Staff

Illustration 14
Implementing and Managing the Plan

Of course, there is the matter of putting all of the above in place and
directing its initial operation. That should, ideally, be part of the staff
development activity and all elements of the plan should be in place at
its conclusion. Continuous monitoring for guiding success is also important. This monitoring can be part of the on-going evaluation of
progress but should be helpful monitoring and not threatening to the
participants.

Evaluation

Evaluation is the final step in the process reported here but should be an on-going process to continue to maintain impetus and improve effectiveness and efficiency as much as possible. There are numerous evaluation models (Provus 1969, Stake 1969, Stufflebeam, 1968) that could be used to evaluate the implementation of technology. However, a generic approach which answers the questions 1. How is the implementation progressing and, 2. What are the effects in terms of the planned and unplanned objectives?

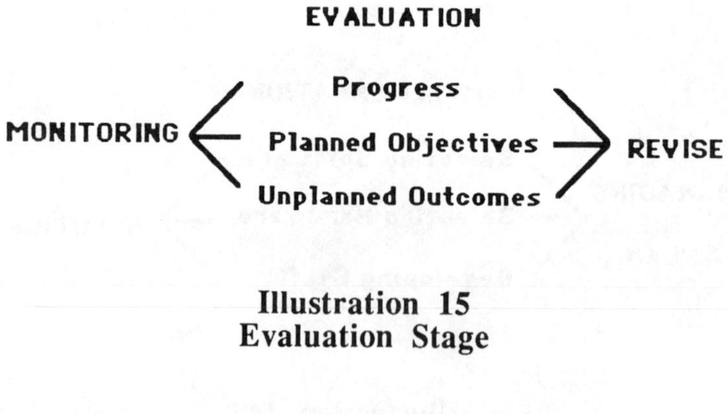

EVALUATION

MONITORING ⟵
Progress
Planned Objectives ⟶ REVISE
Unplanned Outcomes

Illustration 15
Evaluation Stage

Evaluation should take into consideration the progress being made in terms of performing the activities specified in the plan, and in terms of the time lines established for completing tasks. Also, the performance of the tasks should be looked at in terms of their quality and appropriateness. If necessary, changes in the plan or time lines should be made. Evaluation also should consider progress in meeting the objectives previously specified in the planning. If the evidence indicates that the objectives are not being met, changes in the plan may be warranted, again. Finally, good evaluation will seek to uncover benefits not previously anticipated. That is, in retrospect, what other goals or objectives have been met through the implementation. If these are negative outcomes, changes in the plan may need to be made.

Summary

This chapter has presented a systematic approach to managing the implementation of technology in education. The chapter offers an approach which includes the following steps:

1. Establishing Goals
2. Determining Needs
3. Setting Objectives
4. Developing the Solution
5. Managing the Implementation
6. Evaluating the Implementation

These steps are discussed in the chapter and illustrations are shown to symbolize each sub-step in the process. This planning process is a systematic approach to the management of implementation and, if carefully followed, should lead to the attainment of the objectives, improved use of technology, and the improvement of education, in general.

References

Gagne, Robert and Briggs, L.J. *Principles of Instructional Design*. New York: Holt, Rinehart and Winston, 1988.

Harless, J. H. *An Ounce of Analysis*. Newnan, Georgia: Harless Performance Guild, 1975.

Mager, Robert, *Preparing Instructional Objectives*. Palo Alto, California: Fearon Publishers, 1975.

Provus, M. "Evaluation of On-going Programs in the Public School System" in Tyler, R. W. (Ed.). *Educational Evaluation: New Roles, New Means*, The 68th yearbook of the National Society for the Study of Education. Chicago: NSSE, 1969

Stake, Robert. *Needed Concern and Technique for Utilizing More Fully the Potential of Evaluation: New Roles, New Means*, The 68th Yearbook of the National Society for the Study of Education. Chicago, NSSE, 1969

Stufflebeam, Daniel. *Evaluation as Enlightenment for Decision Making*. Columbus, Ohio: Evaluation Center, Ohio State University, 1968.

Tyler, R. W. *Basic Principles of Curriculum and Instruction*. Chicago: University of Chicago Press, 1949.

Suggested Readings

Gagne, Robert and Briggs, L.J. *Principles of Instructional Design*. New York: Holt, Rinehart and Winston, 1974.

Harless, J. H. *An Ounce of Analysis*. Newnan, Georgia: Harless Performance Guild, 1975.

McDaniels, Gary. "Can Computers Improve the Thinking of Students in American Schools?" Link, Frances R. (Ed.), *Essays on the Intellect*, Alexandria, VA: Association for Supervision and Curriculum Development. 1985 (143-150).

Sturdivant, Patricia. "Planning and Training for a New Educational Delivery System." *Educational Leadership* 43 no. 6 (March 1986): 38-39.

Tyler, R. W. *Basic Principles of Curriculum and Instruction*. Chicago: University of Chicago Press, 1949.

Part II

A Planning and Resource Guide

The purpose of Part II of this book is, simply, to provide you with the tools to plan, implement, and evaluate the use of technology in education. By following the steps and procedures suggested, and adding your own creativity, skills and knowledge, you should be assured of a successful entry into, or improvement of, the use of technology and a concomitant improvement in education for your clients, the learners.

Much of what has passed as planning for the use of technology in education has been less than systematic. Most educators would agree that the profession was hit with incredible pressure to 1) improve the learning for youngsters and 2) to increase the use of technology in doing so over the past decade. Many schools quickly ran out and bought equipment in response to this pressure. Unfortunately, that approach seldom works for several reasons. Experience with that approach has shown that:

1. Considerable equipment was purchased that did not work;
2. Equipment was acquired without all necessary components;

3. Equipment purchased was not useful;
4. No one could operate the equipment;
5. Software was overlooked;
6. Equipment was locked up on the shelf; and
7. Numerous other horror stories.

Several worthwhile lessons have been learned over the years and are addressed in Part II of this book. Some of these lessons are:

1. Systematic planning is absolutely essential;
2. Planning must be done by those to be involved;
3. Expert advice is an invaluable resource;
4. Proposed changes must be practical and related to needs;
5. Written aids can be useful for implementation.

These and other problems often encountered in the use of technology in education can be overcome if you follow a plan similar to that presented here in Part II.

Good luck!

Chapter 7
Getting Started

You are ready to begin planning for increased or improved use of technology in your schools! This is an important decision and one which should most certainly result in improved teaching and learning for your charges. The key to success in using technology is similar to that of implementing any change or improvement, doing it carefully and doing it right.

It matters little at this point whether you are an individual or a group. It does not matter, either, if you are a teacher, a principal, or a superintendent of schools. You can implement technological aids with or without great sums of money if you develop and follow a plan similar to the one recommended here. This chapter discusses the initial steps to be taken. Chapter 8 presents further steps for implementation.

Basically, before detailed planning of the solution can be done, you must carefully identify the problem for which you need a solution. Simple as it sounds, this is a very important, even critical, step. Sometimes this step is called a "needs assessment" or a "front-end analysis." By either name, the intent is to identify a problem that needs to be solved prior to planning the solution.

This preliminary analysis involves the identification of your goals, whether those are goals for an institution, a class, or an individual, the determination of which goals are not being met, and an analysis of the reason or reasons why they are not being met. The solution, then, will be addressed directly to correcting these reasons for your goals not being met. This chapter deals with the three steps for identifying the problem.

TIP

> **Individuals who will implement the change or improvement should be directly involved in planning the change.**

Determining Goals

As indicated, the first step is to determine your goals. These goals may already be well established in your school or school system, but a review of those goals for confirmation is still very much in order. In fact, these goals should routinely be reexamined periodically to be sure that they express realistic expectations of the school or school system.

This examination of goals will be a process of creating an awareness of the appropriate purposes for which the schools exist. This should involve an analysis of the mission of the institution and the needs and desires of the individuals who are part of the institution - pupils teachers, administrators, and parents, at a minimum.

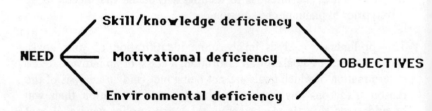

```
                    SETTING OBJECTIVES

                 Skill/knowledge deficiency

    NEED         Motivational deficiency          OBJECTIVES

                 Environmental deficiency
```

Illustration 16
Considerations in establishing goals

The goals define the purpose for the existence and operation of the institution and, really, for everything you do within the institution. Therefore, the goals should be carefully thought out and should represent many different points of view, especially those of pupils, teachers, administrators, and parents.

Establishing a list of goals for an educational institution should not require a major undertaking. There are probably a few feasible ways of conducting this step in the process and you may identify a process that best fits your situation. Some suggested procedures which might assist include the following.

1. Use the forms which appear on the following pages, or produce your own, to conduct a mail survey of appropriate representatives of your school community.

2. Conduct several "open house" type gatherings to discuss the questions specified in the forms on the following pages.

3. Solicit letters from the school community which indicate respondents' perceptions of the strengths and weaknesses of the outcomes of the educational program.

4. Conduct a study, similar to a self-study, of the school or schools, using committees established for that purpose. You may use the forms provided here for guidelines in conducting this study.

5. Ask a consultant to observe in the schools for several days and make a formal written report on the apparent goals of the institution.

6. Conduct a contest for students, one for teachers, one for administrators, and one for parents or others to write an essay on the purpose of your school or system, from their point of view.

Mission, Philosophy, and Goals of

_____**(school name)**

Mission:_____

_____

_____

Philosophy:_____

_____

_____

_____

Goals:_____

_____

_____

_____

(sample)

Mission, Philosophy, and Goals of <u>Metromania Public Elementary</u>

Mission: The mission of the Metromania Elementary school is to prepare its pupils to continue their formal education through the middle and high school grades successfully through the achievement of the basic skills and knowledge of reading, writing, arithmetic, science, and social studies.

Philosophy: The Metromania Elementary School subscribes to the philosophy of Metromania School District of Metromania, KA. We believe that each individual pupil has his or her own unique strengths and weaknesses, the innate ability to learn, and the inalienable right to learn. We also believe that education is first and foremost a humane concern and that pupils should be regarded with dignity and kindness. All possible efforts must be made to allow each individual pupil to become all he or she is capable of being.

Goals: The goals of Metromania Elementary School to which the faculty and staff have subscribed, and which have been approved by the Central Administration and the Board of Education, are as follows.

Graduates of Metromania Elementary School should be able:

1. To read literature written at the sixth grade level upon graduation.
2. To enjoy reading as a leisure time activity.
3. To read to find information for use in solving problems.
4. To use reference materials such as dictionaries, encyclopedias, and the card catalog.
5. To write effectively and correctly.
6. To use written documents to communicate an idea.
7. To use word processing technology to compose written communications.
8. To perform the basic arithmetical operations quickly and accurately.
9. To use modern technology to solve mathematical problems.
10. To understand the decimal number system, including floating point numbers.
11. To understand other number systems, especially the binary system.
12. To know the history of our nation, state, and local community.
13. To appreciate our cultural heritage.
14. To recognize the impact of technology on society in this century.
15. To recognize the geographical diversity of the United States.
16. To recognize the desirability of the cultural diversity of the United States.
17. To understand basic scientific concepts.

State Your Own Goals

by_____Pupil

Things I would like to know about:

Reading :

Writing :

Arithmetic :

Social Studies :

Science :

Determining Needs

Only after the goals are established can you begin to identify real needs. That is because the only needs which can exist are those that result in goals not being met. Therefore, once the goals are established, there should be an analysis of which ones are not being met. This would involve examining all the data possible that pertains to each of the goals listed and arriving at a conclusion about which ones have been met and which ones have not been met.

This can often be accomplished through the use of standardized tests which are routinely administered in schools, but should definitely be supplemented by other measures, as well. Some of the goals which you have specified will, no doubt, not be adequately covered by standardized tests. You might organize your collection and analysis of data using the form on the following page.

Other means of determining which goals have been unmet would most certainly include asking teachers and parents to respond to a questionnaire, developing   and administrating   your own instruments, asking local employers what they believe about the graduates of your schools, or directly inquiring of former students.

You might set up a formal study group to collect and analyze all pertinent data on student achievement in your schools. On a following page is a form which might be useful for collecting a variety of data pertaining to the attainment of each of your goals.

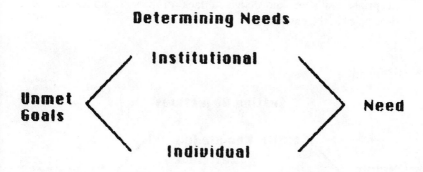

Illustration 17
Identifying Unmet Goals

In many cases, the evidence of unmet goals will be outstanding. In fact, this is desirable from the standpoint of identifying your needs. When an important goal is unmet, the problem is often quite obvious to all concerned. When students are not performing adequately on tests of achievement, for example, the poor performance is not usually a well-kept secret, but is known to many in the school and the community. When graduates leave the schools and go into the work force, employees are not shy to let educators know the weakness among their graduates. Newspapers, likewise, are more than willing to point out the salient deficits in public schools.

Setting Objectives

Once the unmet goals are identified, your problems have been exposed and you can set appropriate objectives to overcome them. This also, however, requires a bit of analysis. Three possible causes might exist which prevent your goals from being met. These are a lack of appropriate skills or knowledge, a lack of proper motivation, or a deficiency in the environment.

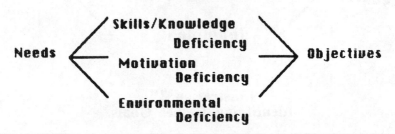

Setting Objectives

Needs < Skills/Knowledge Deficiency / Motivation Deficiency / Environmental Deficiency > Objectives

Illustration 18
Identifying Unmet Needs To Determine Objectives

Goal Attainment Worksheet

Directions: Indicate whether or not each goal has been attained, in your opinion, in the appropriate column and briefly describe the evidence you used in making that judgement.

Attained?

<u>Goal (statement or # from list)</u>   <u>yes/no</u>   <u>Evidence Used</u>

1.
2.
3.
4.
5.
6.
7.
8.
9.
10.
11.
12.
13.
14.
15.
16.
17.
18.
19.
20.
21.

If the cause of the problem is a deficiency of skill or knowledge, then you should investigate further into the basis of these causes. Is the problem one of student performance? If so, is this caused by a deficiency of teacher skill or knowledge? If so, you will need to plan for staff improvement activities to develop the necessary skills and knowledge of the teachers. If not, you will need to further investigate the cause of student performance deficiencies.

The problem, if not a lack of skill or performance, may be one of poor motivation. The lack of proper incentives often results in poor goal attainment. Is there evidence that student performance problems are caused by a lack of motivation? If so, an investigation into how to improve the incentive system is in order.

Finally, if you determine that the source of the problem is due to an environmental deficiency, then you can attack that problem by identifying the exact nature of the deficiency and developing plans for overcoming the problem. This problem may be a lack of resources, equipment, facilities, or improper use of the resources which exist. Perhaps the problem is inadequate skill or knowledge about available resources. In that case, staff development is necessary. Even if the problem is determined to be a lack of resources, staff development may be in order upon the acquisition of additional new resources.

The likelihood is very high that the basic cause of the failure to attain your goals will be a combination of all three: a deficiency of skill and knowledge, poor motivation due to inadequate incentives, and environmental deficiencies. Your further analysis should reveal the real problem and your objectives can be directed toward the solutions.

You will, no doubt, need to survey existing skills and knowledge, current levels of interest, and current resources in your school or school system in order to help you define your objectives. Some sample forms for conducting surveys that deal with the use of technology and which can assist you to develop an appropriate solution to your problem appear on the following pages. These sample survey forms are provided as suggestions for the kind of data you might want to collect before setting your specific objectives for improvement or change.

A few examples of unmet goals and the accompanying analysis of these unmet goals will assist you in setting your objectives for change or improvement.

Unmet Goals	Skills/ Knowledge	Motivation/ Incentive Deficiency	Environmental Deficiency
To write effectively	1. Inability to sequence a series of thoughts. 2. Poor writing skills.	None	1. Inadequate time. 2. Inadequate facilities
To perform basic arithmetic operations.	Do not remember facts.	None	Lack of teacher time.
To report student progress effectively, efficiently, and on time.	None	None	Inadequate equipment

Analysis of Unmet Goals

This further analysis, which must be done, reveals some additional causes of the problems cited. These causes, then, are the ones which must be addressed by your objectives and solution strategies.

Inventory of Current Use of Educational Technology in _____School

Name of Respondent:_____Title:_____

Please use this form to report any use you are currently making of educational technology in your work. The purpose of this inventory is to determine which resources are available in this (school)(school system) and the numbers of persons making use of these applications. Please include any of the following, or other, types of technology which you use.

___Microcomputers and software ___ Data bases ___ Data processing

___ Videodisc or videotape___Word processors(ing)___ Spread sheets

___ Programmed instruction ___ Test scoring or scanning devices

___Computer assisted instruction ___Test generators

___Voice synthesis ___ Photographics or graphics

Name of application or device:_____

Type of Use:__Instructional__Instructional Support __Administrative

Subject areas in which used(if appropriate): _____

Grade level at which used (if appropriate): _____

Objectives for which used:_____

Hardware required:_____

Software required:_____

Cost: Special features:

Special student population for which appropriate:

Hardware Inventory for _____School

Please list on this form any equipment presently in your school building regardless of whether or not it is currently being used.

Type of Equipment:

Make/Model/Description: Capacity:

Accessories and Peripherals:

Condition and approximate age:

Level of current use: none, light(less than 2 hrs/wk.), heavy(5-10 hrs/wk.), Very heavy (10 hrs. plus)

Location in building:

Number of pieces on hand:

Software and Courseware Inventory for_____School

Please include all software which is in your school and which is used with a modern delivery system such as a computer, videotape or disc player, auto-tutorial device, or other self-instructional device.

Name of software:

Type of software: ___Instructional ___Support ___Administrative

Description:

If instructional, type: __Self-Instructional __Drill & Practice __Tutorial __Simulation __Problem Solving __Record Manager __Testing __About Computers or Computing __Other.

Apparent or Stated Objectives:
Special Features:
Cost: Hardware required:

Survey of Skills and Knowledge

Faculty

Name:_____

School:_____

1. I use computers in my teaching

A. Never
B. Seldom
C. Sometimes
D. Often
E. All the time

2. I am skillful at using

A. Instructional Applications (CAI, Tutorial, etc.)
B. Instructional Support Applications (Record Keeping,   Testing, etc.)
C. Administrative Applications(Scheduling, Inventory, Permanent Records, etc.)
D. Standard Packages (Word Processing, Data Base, Spread Sheets, Graphics, etc.)
E. None of the above

3. I can operate the following equipment effectively

A. Computer (list types):
B. Intelligent Video Equipment
C. Digital Plotters
D. Usual audio-visual equipment
E. None of the above

4. I am knowledgeable about

A. History of technology
B. Equipment operations
C. Software
E. Social impact of technology
F. None of the above

5. I am skillful at

A. Programming (list languages):
B. Operations (list equipment):
C. Teaching utilization (of what technologies?):
D. Evaluating software
E. None of the above

6. I have studied the following topics

A. Instructional design
B. Technology in teaching
C. Designing computer applications for instruction
D. Evaluating software
E. Programming computers

7. I have used computers for

A. Teaching subjects (list subjects):
B. Teaching about computers
C. Personal use (correspondence, record keeping, etc.)
D. Business use
E. Other (please list):

8. I believe the greatest potential for technology in education is

A. Administrative use
B. Instructional use
C. Instructional support functions
D. Personal use by teachers
E. None of the above

9. I am familiar with the following instructional uses of computers

A. Drill and practice
B. Tutorials
C. Simulations and/or games
D. Problem solving
E. Computer literacy
F. None of the above

10. I am familiar with the following instructional support applications

A. Test creation, scoring, recording
B. Instructional materials development using graphics
C. Student record keeping and grade reporting
D. Electronic chalkboard
E. Bulletin boards
F. None of the above

11. I am familiar with the following administrative applications

A. Scheduling
B. Record keeping
C. Budgeting, accounting
D. Inventory control
E. Other (please list):

F. None of the above.

12. I am familiar with the following applications for personal use

A. Word processing
B. Data base
C. Spread sheets
D. Statistics
E. Other (please list):

Survey of Skills and Knowledge

Students

Name:_____

Grade: _____

Class:_____School_____

		Yes	No
1. Do you have a microcomputer at home?		O	O
2. Do you use a microcomputer several days a week?		O	O
3. Can you use word processing software?		O	O
4. Do you know what "telecommunications" means?		O	O
5. Have you ever seen a videodisc display?		O	O
6. Have you ever received special help with any subject in school from a computer?		O	O
7. Have you ever taken a course on computers or other educational equipment?		O	O
8. Do you know how to program with a computer language?		O	O
9. Can you use a data base program?		O	O
10. Can you use a spread sheet program?		O	O
11. Do you know what "LOGO" is?		O	O
12. Do you know any of the effects of technology on your life?		O	O
13. Do you know when the first computer was built?		O	O
14. Do you know what is meant by "integrated circuit?"		O	O
15. Have you ever used computer graphics?		O	O
16. Could you write a program to balance a checkbook?		O	O
17. Do you think you will use computers when you grow up?		O	O
18. Are there some things you would like to do with computers?		O	O
19. Would you like to be a computer scientist?		O	O
20. Do you think a microcomputer could help you with schoolwork?		O	O

Summary

This chapter has "walked" you through the first steps in getting ready to develop a plan for using educational technology in your school or schools. This chapter focused on the identification of the problem toward which a technological solution could be addressed.The chapter presented an approach to needs assessment, or front-end analysis which helps you to do the following:

1. To determine your goals;

2. To determine your needs; and

3. To set your objectives.

Several data collection instruments are offered for your consideration in performing these three steps. You may use them as is or adapt them to your needs. You may also choose to develop instruments of your own. In any case, you will benefit from all the data you can collect in reaching the final decision to implement a particular technological solution to your identified problems.

Chapter 8
Developing the Plan

You have conducted your start up activities which should have involved creating an awareness of your institution's goals, individual's goals, and available resources at your disposal. These steps are, indeed, part of the overall plan and you may be developing the plan at the same time as you are conducting the start up activities. If not, you can start this plan from the point of knowing what your important goals are to be for the plan.

Developing the plan involves specifying all of the steps which need to be performed in order to put the solution designed to meet the objectives into effect. The total plan should include:

Awareness of goals

> Institutional
> Individual

Determine needs

> Institutional
> Individual

Setting objectives

> Skills/knowledge
> Motivational
> Environmental

Developing the Solution Plan

Evaluation criteria
Implementation steps

Implementation

Selecting software
Selecting hardware
Developing staff

Evaluation

Progress
Planned objectives
Unplanned outcomes

The first three major steps were discussed in Chapter 7. This chapter deals with the fourth step, developing the solution. This includes the specification of the criteria for the objectives specified and a step-by-step plan for implementation.

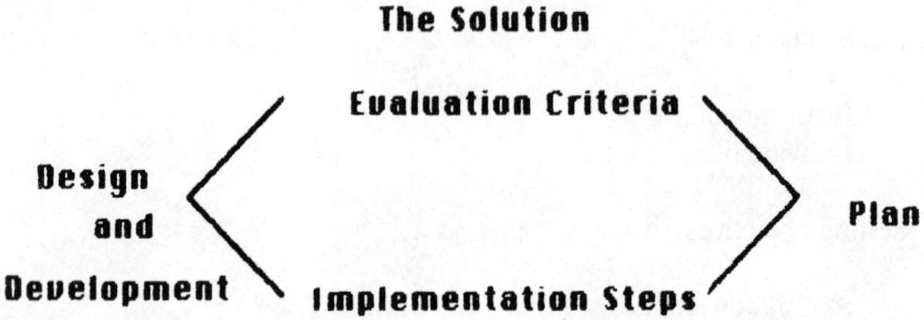

The Solution

Evaluation Criteria

**Design
and
Development**

Plan

Implementation Steps

**Illustration 19
Developing the Solution Plan**

Evaluation Criteria

The first step in any plan of implementation, after the objectives have been set, is to define the criteria for determining progress during and following the implementation. If the objectives are well defined, the task of determining appropriate evaluation criteria will be much easier than if they are vague and/or unclear. Therefore, a little time spent on clarifying your objectives may be an integral part of this step, also.

The evaluation criteria should specify "how will I know when I have met the objective?" Each objective specified should deal with either 1) the acquisition of skills and/or knowledge, 2) improvements in motivation or incentives, or 3) alterations in the environment, especially in terms of resources. Considering the previously cited examples criteria could be indicated as follows.

Cause of problem	Type	Objective	Criteria
Cannot sequence a series of thoughts.	s/k	Increase writing practice under supervision.	Logical essay 1-2 pages.
Writing skills.	s/k	Use correct style.	Correct writing
Lack of time.	en.	Increase time on task.	1 hour / day, supervised
Poor facilities.	en.	Improve conditions for writing.	Word processing.
Arith. facts	s/k	Memorize +,-,x,/ facts	95% correct
Poor data processing.	en.	Improve administrative data processing	Integrated systems.

The criteria presented in the chart above are very briefly stated and need considerable expansion to be fully explanatory. For example, one to three page essays per week to be read carefully by the teacher will be monitored by having the teachers maintain a specially designed record keeping system which identifies the student, the title of the paper, the teacher's comments, and dates of revisions, when necessary. The use of arithmetic drill and practice lessons will be monitored for level of use and through periodic sampling of achievement by students.

Each objective in your plan should be similarly analyzed and the evaluation criteria identified. Staff can begin immediately to develop the data collection instruments that you will use during and after implementation. The next step is to lay out the detailed plan for implementation.

Implementation Steps

In Chapter 6 the use of a planning aid was suggested. The purpose of such an aid is to present, in capsulated form, the activities, events, times, and critical sequences to be followed in implementing a plan. Whether you choose to use such an aid, or merely to list or outline the steps you propose using, you need to be specific, to show deadlines, and to show relationships between various steps. Indicating personnel who are responsible for steps in the plan, dates, and benchmarks are all helpful indicators to gauge your implementation efforts.

In order to develop the plan you need to begin with the first objective and spell out the sequence of events, the time-line for performing the events, and who is to do what, and when. If, for example, you have concluded that the causal factors leading to your problems cited above could be addressed by a new tutorial laboratory and a new administrative system, you would plan the steps for those solutions. Your plan for these objectives might appear as follows.

Objective	Event	Activity	Dates	Who
Tutorial	Specifications	Study	Sept-Dec	Teachers
Lab	Send RFB's	Write/mail	Jan	Admin.
	Receive bids	Review	Mar-Apr	Committee
	Request demos	Review	May	All
	Order		Jun-Aug	Admin.
	Install		Aug	Vendors
	Staff development	Workshop	Aug	Curr. Dir.
	Monitor use	Supervise	Sep-Jun	Curr. Dir
Adminis-	Specifications	Study	Sept	Admin.
trative	Send RFB's	Write/mail	Oct	Staff
System	Receive bids	Review	Dec	Committee
	Select	Evaluate	Jan	Committee
	Order		Jan	Admin.
	Install		Feb	Vendor
	Train staff	OJT	Feb-Mar	Vendor

These activities, events, and dates can be presented as is, above, or in another format such as the one that appears in Illustration 12 on page 60. Or, they can be further described through a narrative description. The reason for planning the steps in considerable detail is, of course, to know in advance who is to do what, how, when, and where.

One useful way to be sure to include everything that must be done is to separate your immediate objectives from the longer-range ones. The immediate objectives are ones which:

1. Are of immediate concern;

2. Can be implemented within a year;

3. Are known to work;

4. Are readily available;

5. Are affordable;

6. Can be implemented with available resources;

7. Can be upgraded (or improved) at a later time;

8. Address an educational need, such as:
   A. Instructional Improvement;

   B. Instructional Management Support Improvement;

   C. Administrative Improvement;

Long-range goals, on the other hand, should be more concerned with continued improvements and the support and maintenance of the implementation during the early phases. Long-range goals are ones which:

1. Address continued evaluation of short-range goals;

2. Deal with continued improvements;

3. Address changes based upon revised needs;

4. Address continued utilization;

5. Consider support systems for continued utilization.

6. Provide for a continuous review process.

In addition to having short-range objectives and long-range goals, some factors which should be considered in developing the implementation plan are:

_ Where will new equipment and software be located?

_ Who will be responsible for operation and maintenance?

_ What will be the hours of operation of labs, clinics, etc.?

_ Who will be allowed to use new facilities?

_ How will software be distributed, managed, and upgraded?

_ How will facilities, equipment, and software be secured?

_ How will staff be trained to effectively use the facilities?

_ What incentives will be provided for effectiveness?

A worksheet for specifying the steps in the plan for implementation appears on the next page.

Developing the Plan

State the Performance Objective:_____

_____

_____

State the Evaluation Criteria:_____

_____

_____

Identify Methods of Collecting Information:_____

_____

_____

Identify Instruments for Evaluation:_____

_____

_____

Set Dates for:
Completing Evaluation Plan:_____ Starting Data Collection:_____
Complete Data Collection:_____ Begin Analysis:_____
Complete Analysis:_____
Complete the following:

Who?   Does What?   When?

_____

_____

You will probably want to include a list of events and activities.

Summary

This chapter has been addressed to the development of a plan for implementing a change in schools that involves the use of technology. The overall plan involves all the steps described here in Part II, but the plan discussed in this chapter includes setting the evaluation criteria for monitoring progress and defining the steps to be taken in the actual implementation. The preceding chapter, Chapter 7, discusses the steps involved in getting started and Chapters 9, 10, and 11 deal with the steps of selecting hardware, selecting software, and developing staff, respectively.

Chapter 9
Selecting Hardware

To implement the plan of action, requires very careful selection of hardware, software, and the development of staff performance competencies. This chapter focuses on the selection of appropriate hardware for meeting the objectives of the plan. Comparing, evaluating, selecting, and purchasing hardware is one of the most interesting aspects of starting a program which uses educational technology. However, it is a task which can be full of dangerous pitfalls which, in turn, lead to disastrous results. These pitfalls can only be avoided through careful and thoughtful planning.

Most everyone has heard of a least one instance in which a school system spent considerable sums of money for equipment which was never used. This unfortunate experience is usually due to either:

The system did not work at all;

The system did not do what it was acquired to do;

Some essential components (software, peripheral device) were not acquired or available; or

No one could figure out how to operate the system.

Fortunately, these inadequacies or failures can be avoided through careful planning and management, especially in the step of selecting hardware and software, and training staff to operate the systems. Four key suggestions for selecting hardware can help enormously to avoid these problems.

1. Know what the hardware is supposed to do;

2. Become familiar with the state-of-the-art in educational technology;

3. Specify selection criteria in advance of considering alternatives;

4. Compare available systems which meet the criteria.

Each of these steps is discussed in this chapter along with some aids for carrying them out. The results of following these steps will be most beneficial if you proceed with reasonable care and specify short-term objectives and long-term goals.

Illustration 20
Implementing and Managing the Plan

Know What the Hardware is Supposed to Do

In order to judge whether or not the hardware you are considering even works, you will need to know what the necessary components are and what they are supposed to do. These considerations have all been discussed in Chapter 3, which you might want to review before going on with your hardware selection. To assist you in deciding whether or not you need help in this area, the following checklist could be used as a guide to determine your own, and that of others in the schools, knowledge of hardware and its purposes.

Checklist of Basic Hardware Knowledge

Do you know what the:	Yes	No
1. Central Processing Unit does? Describe (if desired):	O	O
2. Keyboard (input device) does? Describe (if desired):	O	O
3 . Disk drive (or drives) do? Describe (if desired):	O	O
4. Monitor does? Describe (if desired):	O	O
5. Memory does? Describe (if desired):	O	O
6. Cassette player does? Describe (if desired):	O	O
7. Videodisc player does? Describe (if desired):	O	O
8. Videodisc does? Describe (if desired):	O	O

9. Telephone does?   O   O
   Describe (if desired):

10. Telecommunications is?   O   O
    Describe (if desired):

Add any special skills or knowledge which you have:

These questions represent the most important information that you will
need to judge the effectiveness of the hardware you will be examining.
You will also be able to compare alternative systems on these points,
asking questions such as:

   1. What are the relative capacities?

   2. What are the relative speeds?

   3. What are the relative costs?

   4. What are the relative expected lifespans (durability) of the
   components?

   5. What is the relative ability for expansion?

   6. What is the relative compatibility with other systems?

   7. What is the relative ability to use existing software which is
   needed?

Become Familiar with the State-of-the-Art

Even though you might be thoroughly knowledgeable with the basic
components of various systems, and their functions, you might need
some updating on the latest developments in hardware. Unless you
read specialty journals on a regular basis, you probably are not com-
pletely up to date, given the rapidity of changes in technology. For example, it is not uncommon for a manufacturer to make an offer you
cannot refuse just before announcing the availability of an updated version of that product. Sometimes, this results in some real bargains.

However, sometimes it results in great disappointment when you discover that in 30 days the system will be available at similar cost with great enhancements. You might have wanted, or needed, those enhancements but were not aware of their pending availability.

There are several ways to stay abreast of current developments in educational technology. You might do any, or all, of the following:

_ Join one of the professional societies listed in the appendix.

_ Attend at least one conference per year of a professional society.

_ Join a "Users' Group" usually of users of similar hardware.

_ Join and participate in one or more bulletin board services.

_ Make a point to regularly talk with colleagues who are known as "Buffs."

_ Subscribe or obtain journals on educational technology which are listed in the appendix.

_ Read popular computing magazines listed in the appendix.

These are some of the ways of remaining up-to-date. There are real advantages to visiting computer stores and letting the management know you are interested in purchasing some hardware. Local universities and colleges may have laboratories with the latest equipment for demonstration. Manufacturing representatives are usually willing to visit and conduct demonstrations, as well. Be creative, dig a little, and you will be amazed at what new products sit on the horizon just waiting to be announced.

Specifying Hardware Selection Criteria

In defining selection criteria, the primary consideration to keep in mind is that the hardware must have the capability to do what you need it to do. This consideration, alone, will narrow your choices somewhat, but you will still have some alternate from which to choose in all likelihood. In making the final choice there are a number of other criteria which you will need to consider. Among the most important factors to consider are:

_ Cost
_ Components included in base price
_ Durability
_ Maintenance support availability
_ Expandability
_ Compatibility
_ Documentation availability and quality
_ Customer service availability and quality
_ Vendor (manufacturer or retailer) reputation
_ Software availability and quality

Cost

Base prices for computer systems, and other technologies, vary considerably. A microcomputer system which meets the description presented in Chapter 3 could cost as little as $700 or as much as $10,000 depending on the brand name and what is included in the base price. Prices will not remain static, however, and the trend has been toward lower costs for many technologies. Unfortunately, no standard prices can be stated at any given time due to the tremendous fluctuations constantly taking place. Special programs have been offered providing as much as a forty percent discount on one brand of microcomputer for educators. What you will need to do is to practice good consumerism by comparison shopping for the best available prices. Under no circumstances should you accept the first offer before making many comparisons of equivalent systems.

Components Included in Base Price

One well known manufacturer delivered a quality system to customers who paid the asking price without an accompanying disk operating system that is (or was) an essential component. Many peoples' eyes were rudely opened when they installed their $5,000 microcomputers to find they could not be used because the disk operating system had not been purchased, or even ordered. This tends to be changing, however, and most systems come ready to use, some even with batteries in place. Nevertheless, various manufacturers and/or retail stores will offer systems with some add-ons at the base price. Things to look for in your shopping include 80 column capability for both screen and printer, memory size (512K has become almost standard), number of disk drives included (one is essential, two are very useful), color monitors, modem, and graphics facilities for microcomputers. Other technologies such as satellite receiving dishes and video players do not come with nearly as many options, though their prices can vary just as much. Again, it is a shopper's market and you will need to comparison shop as much as you can to get the best buys.

Durability

Durability - a strong word - means a lot when evaluating technologies. In some cases durability of technology can be life saving, such as with space technology. Durability of educational technology is mostly applicable to the ability of the hardware to withstand the rigors of use by young enthusiasts. One teacher, who works in the back woods of Alaska, refers to one popular brand of microcomputer as "bullet-proof." He has literally trucked his microcomputers into and out of the back woods of Alaska, over hill and dale so to speak, set them up cold and operated them off small, local, generators for more than five years with practically no failures. That is an incredible record, but one which you should look for in equipping your schools. Such a record is not unattainable, as witnessed by the teacher from Alaska. Of course, all vendors will claim durability! Your best bet is to talk to colleagues who have similar schools and find out about the track record of the equipment they have been using.

Maintenance Support and Quality

The same vendor that failed to supply a disk operating system delivered three $5,000 microcomputers to a customer who excitedly set them up the same day. Lo and behold, only one of the three worked. The customer called the vendor, in some state of panic, and was told to pack the systems in the original boxes and deliver them back to the store. Imagine, $5,000 per system and the customer was told to return them to the store, himself! In that case, the problem turned out to be a simple replacement of two malfunctioning interface cards which could have easily been replaced on site. Other vendors, on the other hand, will go to nearly any length to support the customer with maintenance, including providing pickup and delivery, free loaners while the faulty equipment is being repaired, and trouble shooting over the telephone to help the customer make their own repairs. The only way to find out about the level and quality of maintenance support available to you is to ask and to compare with other vendors and check with other customers about their experiences.

Expandability

You may want to consider the capability of any hardware to accept added capability. Added capability can be attained by adding components to the basic system after you have acquired the system. Components which can usually be added include expanded memory, eighty column cards, graphics facilities, color monitors, alternative input devices, sound synthesizers, additional disk drives, and multi-media equipment. Of special importance is the ability to add random access memory.

Compatibility

There are really two kinds of compatibility. One is the ability of a system to run all the software of another brand. The other, perhaps more important even, is the record of the manufacturer to produce upgrades which will continue to run software developed for, or on, older versions of the same brand. The first type of compatibility is easy to determine: simply ask for a demonstration. The second type of compatibility can only be determined through the past history of the manufacturer.

Documentation

Is documentation supplied that fully explains to users everything they need to know about using the system? User documentation has traditionally been known to be readable only to those who already know the hardware. Today's systems are used by everybody, and the documentation should enable nearly everyone to make use of the equipment. You may want to call on some users from your own school system to help with the evaluation of the available documentation.

Customer Service Availability and Quality

This service goes beyond that offered for maintenance support. Some vendors offer extensive assistance with staff training, either at your site or theirs. They may also provide follow-up visitation to assure effective utilization and to make suggestions for improvement or upgrading or maintenance of your system. You can only ascertain the vendors intention in this regard by asking and by checking with other customers about their experiences.

Vendor Reputation

The reputation of the vendor with whom you are talking is not difficult to ascertain - it is all in it's history. You can ask anyone who has had dealings with the vendor about its reputation. Has the vendor abruptly discontinued a model leaving the former customers on their own? Does the vendor drop the customer as soon as the deal is closed? Is the vendor concerned with your success with the purchase? These and other questions pertaining to the vendor's reputation can be asked of anyone who has previously dealt with the vendor. They will usually be happy to tell you of their experience, be it good or bad.

Software Availability

Some brands of equipment have extensive software but it applies to a special area such as business or industry. You are interested in specific applications for instruction, instructional support, or school management and administrative applications. You can inquire about this and request catalogs and demonstrations. Or, you can read some of the journals listed in the appendix and reach you own conclusion of how much software is available. This does not address the quality of the software, but quantity, alone, is an important consideration. Is there sufficient software available from which you can pick and choose?

These criteria, plus others which may be important to you should be considered in making your choice of hardware. Essentially, this can be done with a simple checklist similar to the one which appears on a following page.

Comparing Available Systems

In comparing available systems, you will probably have to make your objectives well known to the community, or at least the local vendor representatives. If considerable money is in the offing, the vendors will flock to your door with offers of demonstrations, trials, etc. If little money is expected, you may have to do the leg work yourself by calling on the vendors at their locations. However, you probably should first try to get the vendor out to your site to get a better view of your needs.

If the vendors have employees who are knowledgeable about education, they can be very helpful in suggesting alternatives. Ask for the assistance of such people when you call the vendor representative. Tell them or, better yet, show them your plans to this point including a good definition of your needs and objectives. Let them make the pitch to you about the particular system that will meet your needs. Share with them, if you wish, the checklist similar to the one on the next page which you are using in making your evaluation. Above all, use such a checklist and ask the sales person to respond to the items which you think are important.

Checklist of Specifications for Educational Equipment

Name of System_____

Name of Vendor:_____ _____

Type of Equipment:_____ _____

= =

Directions: Indicate the level of availability and quality of each of the criteria according to the following scale: 5 = excellent, 4 = very good, 3 = satisfactory, 2 = acceptable, 1 = unacceptable.

= =

1. Meets specified purpose or objective.	5 4 3 2 1
2. Components included.	5 4 3 2 1
3. Durability	5 4 3 2 1
4. Maintenance.	5 4 3 2 1
5. Expendability.	5 4 3 2 1
6. Compatibility.	5 4 3 2 1
7. Documentation.	5 4 3 2 1
8. Customer service.	5 4 3 2 1
9. Vendor reputation.	5 4 3 2 1
10. Software availability.	5 4 3 2 1
11. Other	5 4 3 2 1

Total____

Chapter 10
Selecting Software

Selecting software is a very important aspect of your overall plan to use technology in education. In fact, next to the staff development program which is to be provided, the selection of software is the most important thing you will do for the ultimate goal of improving education in your school or school system.

Software, the written, programmed, or coded instructions for using any technology, is the key to success. All the pots and pans and measuring utensils in the world cannot produce a fine devil's food cake! Even with automatic dispensers of exact quantities of ingredients (although this, too, requires a program or recipe) cannot produce a fine cake without other instructions. The software, on the other hand, might work just as well on several pieces of equipment or manually.

Software, then, should be selected based upon the function it is to serve. Then, the hardware which seems to be best suited to the software can be selected. If the hardware is already in place, in addition to considering the functional needs for software, you will need to be sure that it will operate properly on existing equipment. In either case, the selection of software is crucial to success, and much care should be taken with this process.

This chapter offers a procedure, along with appropriate materials for reviewing, evaluating, acquiring, and disseminating software. You may use the criteria and evaluation forms presented in this chapter or you may adapt them to suit your unique situation.

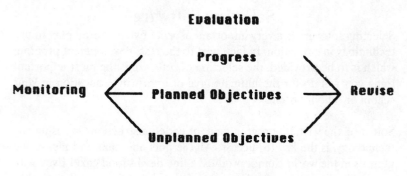

Illustration 21
Evaluation Stage

Specifying Software Criteria

Criteria which can be used for selecting software can also be used for creating original software. However, since so much software is readily available at reasonable prices, that prospect will not be discussed here. Rather, you should concentrate on creating a list of criteria for selecting software which suits your situation.

There is, in fact, an overabundance of software available today. Unfortunately, the quality of this software varies tremendously, from programs which do not even "run" to programs which may surpass all of your dreams. The variability of the quality of software on the market today makes it essential that minimal criteria be established by the consumer, and not left up to the word of the producers. Several basic areas for which you might want to set standards for software include compatibility with program needs, subject matter coverage, appropriateness for audience, effective and efficient operations, instructional design characteristics, duplication restrictions, and compatibility with your hardware.

Compatibility with Program Needs

The first criteria for selecting software should be its appropriateness for a specific need in your school or schools system. More than one solution to a problem is usually available. Therefore, the solutions being examined should be compared for both effectiveness and efficiency in terms of your specific need or problem. For example, a need for word processing in the curriculum may well call for a solution other than that which would serve the need for word processing in the administrative office. Whereas Bank Street Writer might be very appropriate for teaching word processing to young children, a system such as *Word Perfect, Word Star*, or *Applewriter II* might be more appropriate for the office.

Subject Matter

As with any delivery system (textbook, film, statistics, etc.) there should be a real concern with the fidelity of the content with what is known in the field. Errors in content will inevitably occur whatever the medium of delivery, however, accuracy and fidelity should be of major concern. Additionally, the content presented should be the content which you want in your curriculum! Remember, software is created by humans, and individuals who write courseware may interpret content differently than someone else. Your task is to be sure that the content fits your needs.

Also, the content covered should be broad enough in scope to meet your curricular needs. Short, isolated pieces of instruction may not be very useful to you unless it meets an isolated need for a specific item of instruction. More comprehensive courseware would, logically, be more useful for larger numbers of students.

The same principle applies to administrative or instructional support software, as well. A scheduling program which does not suit your particular scheduling needs, would not be very useful to you. Or, a test generating program which produces only one type of test item might not fit with your policy of testing. The fidelity of the software to the your problem is an essential consideration.

Compatibility with Targeted Users

Fundamentally, the software must be usable by the individuals for whom it is acquired. With curricular software, of course, the primary consideration is its appropriateness for the curriculum being taught at the grade level selected. In addition, however, all software should be readable by the users, and should not tax them to the point of frustration or, at the other extreme, should not insult the average user's intelligence, either.

Operations

You might be surprised at how simple some of the criteria for the operational characteristics of software might need to be. Several specific factors pertaining to simple operations must be considered.

_ Does the software work? Incredibly, this question must be asked! Software does not always work as advertised, or work at all.

TIP

Do Not Purchase Software Sight Unseen!

Check out the software carefully, either at the store or in your own facility before committing to purchase. If that is impossible, get the name of someone who has purchased the software from the seller, and contact that individual or school.

_ Is the software easy to use? The ease of use of software varies tremendously. There really is no good reason for it to be difficult or sometimes, nearly impossible for the average person to use any given software. Software today is becoming very "user friendly" and you do not need to settle for software that requires a system analyst to operate it.

_ Is the software durable: This is very difficult to judge, but try to get some estimate of how much use can be expected of the software. Check

on how well it is protected from vandalism or careless use. One definition of durability that is heard is: "A bulletproof program is one which
cannot be easily crashed by a hyperactive third grader or three aggres-
sive first graders in less than one minute" (author unknown). For that
matter, any user who receives the error message, "You have found an
error, please notify the manufacturer, "will quickly become frustrated if
money was paid for the software.

_ What are the hardware requirements? Be sure that the software will
work with the equipment you have or are planning to purchase.
Memory needed, number of disk drives, output devices such as
printers, color screens or voice synthesizers, to mention a few, should
be specified so that the software purchased will work properly on your
system.

_ Is the software adaptable? You might want to consider the possibility
of altering software through your own programming efforts. This can
be done with much available software, but not all. If this is important,
the capability should be determined in advance.

_ Is the software well documented? There should always be accompanying literature (documentation) which explains how to use the
software, what is needed to use it , and what its system characteristics
(languages, utilities, special features) are.

Copying Policy

Generally, software is protected by U.S. Copyright laws. Some
software, such as that called Public Domain, is not so protected. You
need to know what policy covers the software being considered. Can
the software be duplicated for each school, or must a separate copy be
purchased? If you purchase one for each school, can you duplicate it
for separate classes? At a minimum, does the producer give you the
right to make one back-up copy? You will need to know the policy
before you make the purchase to avoid legal conflicts.

Instructional Design Features

If the software is being considered for use as an instructional tool,
several additional criteria should be considered. Many of these criteria

would also apply to instructional support and administrative software, but they are critical for instructional software.

_Are the objectives clearly stated? The objectives should be stated, but they may be simply inferred. The user should be able to readily identify the objectives, however, and they should fit the learning need at hand.

_Are the individual screen displays attention getting? Good screens are attractive, easy to read, interesting, and motivating. Screens merely filled with text may be boring and distracting. Graphic displays are usually appropriate.

_Does the content refer to prior learning? Learning may proceed best when it builds upon something already known. Stimulating the recall of the prerequisite learning is desirable.

_ Does the program require much interaction from the learner? One key to learning is to provide ample opportunities for responding to the learning material. Simply pressing the return key or the space bar to continue the flow of text is not adequate for interactive learning.

_ Does the program provide immediate feedback, both reinforcing and corrective? Following each response from the learner, the program should present either reinforcement or corrective feedback to the learner.

_ Does the program provide every opportunity for the correct response? The learner should be given ample opportunity to respond correctly. Time limits and restrictions on number of tries should be kept to a minimum.

_Does the program provide help screens or routines? Part of providing opportunities for success is the provision of help routine which the user can access quickly and easily.

_Does the program provide records of learners' activities and performance? A good instructional program should provide information on each learner's progress and also summative data on groups or classes.

_Does the user have adequate control of the program? In some cases you may want the learner to have control, in other cases you may not. Perhaps the best provision would be for you, the teacher, to be able to determine who controls the program.

Reviewing Software

Reviewing software usually requires that at least a sample of the software be acquired to be reviewed first hand. It would be wise to acquire such software as inexpensively as possible because of the risk of its being inappropriate for your needs. This is complicated by a frequent reluctance on the part of producers of software to provide free samples due to the fear that the recipient will duplicate the software and return the sample. This might be avoided by offering to sign an agreement to not copy any sample software.

Other ways of avoiding the problem of viewing software first hand involve getting the vendors to demonstrate their products. This can be done by visiting the store showroom or by inviting sales people to visit your school. Vendors seem to enjoy bringing their products out to the schools if enough potential buyers will show up for the demonstration. This may be accomplished by holding a computer fair and inviting several school districts to attend.

At a minimum, you would be well advised to at least talk first hand with some other users of the software. Ask the vendor to supply you with a list of those who have acquired the software in question. Telephone or visit these locations and talk with the users and, perhaps, see a demonstration of a live use of the software.

Evaluating Software

Once you are in front of the software to be considered, refer back to your criteria for evaluation. On the following page is a checklist which contains the criteria presented above. You may use this as a checksheet, as a rating scale, or adapt it for your own purposes. The main point to be made here is to collect as much information as you can in the time available to you. In a rather short time you will find your school to be in possession of considerable software. Being selective at this point can save you much money and considerable time later on.

Courseware Evaluation Form

Name of Software Program_____

Sold by_____**of**_____

Seller's Address_____

Computer System Required_____

Additional Requirements_____

_____

<u>Check Off</u>	<u>Criteria</u>	Rating*
_____	1. Meets the curriculum or learning needs identified.	5 4 3 2 1
_____	2. Subject matter is adequate and correct.	5 4 3 2 1
_____	3. Software works as intended.	5 4 3 2 1
_____	4. Software is easy to use.	5 4 3 2 1
_____	5. Software is durable.	5 4 3 2 1
_____	6. Hardware requirements compatible with plans.	5 4 3 2 1
_____	7. Software is easily adaptable.	5 4 3 2 1
_____	8. Documentation.	5 4 3 2 1
_____	9. Copying policy.	5 4 3 2 1
_____	10. Objectives clearly stated.	5 4 3 2 1
_____	11. Attractiveness of screen displays.	5 4 3 2 1
_____	12. Reference to prior skills or knowledge.	5 4 3 2 1
_____	13. Learner interaction with content.	5 4 3 2 1
_____	14. Reinforcement and corrective feedback.	5 4 3 2 1
_____	15. Immediacy of feedback.	5 4 3 2 1
_____	16. Opportunities for success.	5 4 3 2 1
_____	17. Help screens or routines.	5 4 3 2 1
_____	18. Performance recording.	5 4 3 2 1
_____	19. Program control.	5 4 3 2 1

*Scale: 5 = excellent , 4 = very good, 3 = average, 2 = fair, 1 = poor

Acquiring Software

Software for educational use is available from many sources. A list of suppliers is provided in Appendix J of this book. You may order software directly from these, and other, suppliers or you may rely on local stores and/or suppliers to obtain needed software for you. An advantage of using the mail to order software (and supplies) is often a lower price. However, an advantage of using local suppliers is that they will usually back up their sales more readily or, at least, quicker and more easily.

Software is often put on sale for educators and educational institutions. You might benefit by inquiring about this when obtaining ordering information. Sometimes, shopping in the same places for software results in the practice of discounting prices to regular customers, as well.

You will need to order sufficient copies of most software, and sufficient types of software programs, to make the use of technology worthwhile. Isolated bits and pieces of software will not encourage anyone to make use of what is available. Libraries, in fact, need to be established and maintained to make access easy and convenient.

Disseminating Software

Having software available is not the same as its being used. An effort must be made to disseminate the software throughout the school and/or school district. This might be accomplished by a media specialist, a librarian, or a technology coordinator. Whoever is responsible for dissemination should also be given responsibility for maintaining updates to software owned and to updating the collection, as well as getting the software out where it is needed.

Frequently, dissemination is greatly aided by identifying key people in each school and grade to try out new software. This person should be someone who will, indeed, use the software and will share the experience with others. This process of dissemination should be thoughtfully and carefully planned and monitored. Key personnel might also be asked to serve on software advisory committees and to share responsibility for teaching others to use existing and new software.

Summary

This chapter has attempted to provide you with assistance in selecting and using software for educational problems. The chapter includes aids for developing software selection criteria, for obtaining software for review purposes, for evaluating software, for acquiring it, and for disseminating it throughout the school or school district. This step is an extremely important one which may well determine the success or failure of any attempt to improve education through the use of technology.

Chapter 11
Staff Development

The development of staff competencies for the use of educational technology is essential for success of any program. In fact, staff training might be the most important ingredient in the plan to use technology in education. Without adequate training, no plan of action, however good it is, will be successful.

There should be a written plan for the staff development activities which specify the competencies to be acquired, the criteria for knowing when they are acquired, the topics to be presented, the hands — on activities to be provided, and a schedule of sessions. The plan should provide for regular staff development rather than a one-time presentation.

TIP

Involve those who are to be trained in the planning of the staff development program. Try to build a feeling of "ownership" among the trainees by offering incentives, where possible!

This chapter will help you to create a staff development plan. Worksheets and suggestions are provided to assist in the process in the order described above. These can be used as is or modified to suit your unique situation.

Illustration 22
Implementing and Managing the Plan

Competencies Needed

Educators need skills and knowledge about technology and how to teach about technology. Teaching skills will be assumed, however, on the grounds that if the participants are already practicing educators, they possess these skills. The competencies listed here, therefore, are confined to technology, not teaching.

The competencies needed are in the categories of hardware, software, programming, and social impact. You may want to include other categories such as application packages as a special sub-category of software. It should not be assumed that none of the staff to be trained possesses any of the competencies listed, however. For that reason, a survey is suggested as a second step after the specification of competencies to determine which ones are lacking. Following is the list of competencies.

Hardware Competencies

_ To identify, by name and function, the essential parts of any computer system.

_ To select appropriate hardware for an application to solve a given problem.

_ To operate all essential components of at least one computer system.

_ To know the maintenance requirements of at least one computer system.

_ To use documentation(manuals) to learn functions of at least one computer system.

_ To describe at least five alternate peripheral devices and their functions.

Software Competencies

_ To know which resources to use to obtain information about available software.

_ To recognize high quality software from low quality software.

_ To select software suitable for solving a given problem.

_ To use documentation (manuals) to learn how to operate any software package.

_ To organize and maintain software so that it remains accessible and usable.

Programming Competencies

_ To clarify and state a problem in clear and unambiguous terms.

_ To write a step-by-step solution(algorithm) to solve a given or stated problem.

_ To translate the algorithm into an appropriate code such as a flow chart.

_ To convert a flow chart, or other suitable code, into a programming language.

_ To modify computer code in an existing application program.

Social Impact Competencies

_ To list five ways in which technology has affected life in the past 50 years.

_ To identify at least five applications of technology in today's society.

_ To describe the "miracle" of the microchip.

_ To identify at least three major milestones in the history of technology.

Who Needs Which Competencies?

The next step, after specifying *your* list of competencies is to determine who needs training for which competencies. This can be accomplished in several ways. Staff can be asked to respond to questionnaires or checklists, staff can be observed in a laboratory or classroom by qualified personnel or, a random sample of staff may be surveyed where the staff is extremely large. Any of these techniques can be facilitated by a simple form such as appears on the following page. This form may be reproduced and used as is or modified to suit your unique situation.

Computer Skills and Knowledge Inventory

Name_____Date_____School_____

Grade or Subject_____

Directions: In order to meet your needs for staff development for using new technology, we would like you to provide information in response to the items below. Please darken the circle which best represents your level of skill or knowledge and indicate those areas where you would like more assistance.

Competency	Skill/Knowledge			Need Help?	
	Hi	Med.	Low	Yes	No
1. Identifying parts of a computer system.	O	O	O	O	O
2. Selecting hardware components and systems.	O	O	O	O	O
3. Operating relevant equipment.	O	O	O	O	O
4. Knowledge of equipment maintenance requirements.	O	O	O	O	O
5. Using system documentation.	O	O	O	O	O
6. Knowledge of available peripheral devices.	O	O	O	O	O
7. Knowledge of sources of currently available software.	O	O	O	O	O
8. Evaluating software applications packages.	O	O	O	O	O
9. To use documentation for application programs.	O	O	O	O	O
10. Knowledge of software maintenance.	O	O	O	O	O

11. Identifying and stating problems.   O   O   O   OO

12. Creating step-by-step solutions
    to problems.   O   O   O   OO

13. Using and creating flow charts.   O   O   O   OO

14. Programming in a high level language
    such as BASIC.   O   O   O   OO

15. Modifying or fixing existing programs.   O   O   O   OO

16. Knowledge of effects of technology
    in this century.   O   O   O   O.O

17. Knowledge of ways technology is
used today.   O   O   O   OO

18. Knowledge of microtechnology.   O   O   O   OO

19. Knowledge of the history of
modern technology.   O   O   O   OO

20. Knowledge of current trends in
educational technology.   O   O   O   OO

THANK YOU FOR YOUR ASSISTANCE!

TOPICS

For the staff development program, you will certainly need to address topics in all four areas described above: hardware, software, programming, and social impact. There may well be additional topics which are relevant to a local situation which you wish to add to your staff development plans. The four, or more, major topics will also need to be further defined and made locally relevant for each local school or school system. One suggested outline of topics which may be used, or adapted for use, appears on the following page. First, however, some useful TIPS for each of the four categories of topics.

Hardware

> **Begin the staff development activities with easy to use hardware and include as much hands-on opportunities as possible as early as possible in the training!**

Software

> **Begin with an application that is extremely easy to use, is non-threatening, and which can be immediately used by the participants in their own work environment!**

Programming

> **Begin with a simple problem such as making a casserole dish, converting fahrenheit to centigrade, converting the decimal numbers 1 to 25 to binary equivalents, converting numbers from Standard measures to Metric measures, or steps in wrapping a package for the U.S. Mail.**

Social Impact

> **Begin by demonstrating exciting current applications such as videodisc programs.**

Suggested Topical Outline for Staff Development

I. Introduction

   A. Terminology

   B. Hands-On Use

   C. Concepts

II. Technology for Today's Living

   A. Computers
      1. Use of computers in education

      2. Operation of component parts - disk, keyboard.

   B. Videodisc applications
      1. Use in education

      2. Operation

   C. Telecommunications use
      1. Use in education

      2. Operations

III. Software

   A. Operating system software

   B. Application programs

   C. Programming languages

IV. Instructional Applications

V. Teacher Support Applications

VI. Administrative Support Applications

VII. Evaluating Software

VIII. Programming

IX. Local Needs for Educational Technology

Activities

Several types of activities can be used for presenting the topics in a manner which facilitates learning. Hands-on activities have been mentioned previously and should be emphasized here. Demonstrations are also very effective, especially if followed by practice exercises. Vendors often have excellent slide-tape presentations about their products which are often available to anyone who asks for them. Lectures and discussions can also be used to present several of the topics shown in the outline presented earlier. The following chart illustrates a few alternatives and topics for which they might be appropriate.

	Hands-On	Demo's	Vendor	Lecture	Discuss	Seminar	Lab
Hardware	X X	X	X			X	
Software	X	XX	XX	X	X	X	
Programming				X	X	XX	XX
Social Impact				XX	XX	XX	

X = appropriate XX = extremely appropriate

Scheduling Staff Development

Scheduling of staff development is no big issue but experience has shown that exposure over short, intense, sessions may be superior to long, infrequent, short sessions. Meeting once a week for a semester seems less useful than meeting every day for three or four days consecutively. Perhaps the best procedure is to be sure that staff members are not attending staff development "on their own time," that many local staff members are used in making demonstrations and presentations, that vendor representatives are widely used, and that participants are sub-grouped for some sessions according to common interests. A form for planning the schedule of activities appears on the following page.

Technology Workshop Scheduling Form

<u>Monday Tuesday Wednesday Thursday Friday</u>

9:00-10:00

10:00-11:00

11:00-12:00

12:00- 1:00

1:00- 2:00

2:00-3:00

3:00-4:00

Chapter 12
Planning Curriculum

This, the final chapter, deals with developing an appropriate curriculum for schools at all levels from the early elementary grades to adult education. Curricula, of necessity, must change from time to time and what is proposed here may be obsolete in a number of years. However, the process for developing the curriculum may be appropriate and viable for some time to come.

Frequently, curriculum developers begin with curriculum models. One of the most popular and widely used such models is that popularized by Tyler (1949). This model involves the formulation of objectives, activities, materials, and evaluation procedures. Tylerian objectives must be behavioral and they must be clear! The objectives are drawn from an analysis of the content to be taught, the characteristics of society to be served, and the needs of the learners. Tylerian objectives, however, can be broader than, say, Magarian (Mager, 1970) objectives and are, hence, somewhat more suitable for curriculum development, and less so for instructional design and development.

The scope and sequence of the curriculum is defined by the content, which is presented in Chapter 5, Part I, of this book. The content for a technology curriculum is described in that chapter as including the topics of hardware, software, programming, and social impact, and at four levels of skills and knowledge, awareness, utilization, production, and specialization. Assistance for further refining this curriculum for your institution is provided in this chapter. Worksheets are provided for defining goals and objectives, activities, materials and evaluation devices for a technology curriculum at various levels. Your task will be to begin with a specific target population and develop the curriculum for that population and any others you serve.

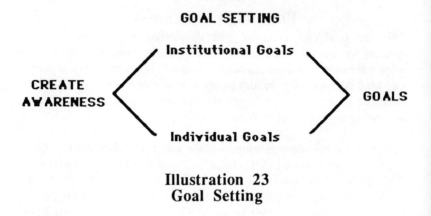

Illustration 23
Goal Setting

Defining Goals and Objectives

Before actually beginning to write your goals and objectives, you should produce a scope and sequence chart similar to that appearing in chapter 5. You might want to be even more specific in terms of the population you serve or the content you want to teach. You can use the form which follows or construct one of your own.

Scope and Sequence of Technology Curriculum

for

Topic: Hardware, Software, Program, Social Impact, Other

Grade:

K _____

1 _____

2 _____

3 _____

4 _____

5 _____

6 _____

7 _____

8 _____

9 _____

10 _____

11 _____

12 _____

Instructions: Fill in the spaces for grade level and topic either with sub-topics to be included in the curriculum or with a check (✓) to indicate that the topic will be included at that grade level or levels.

Beginning with one topic from the scope and sequence chart and developing objectives at an appropriate grade level, you may proceed through a single grade level on all topics or a single topic at all grade levels. The best approach might be to have teams working on either all topics for a single grade level or each topic for every grade level.

Objectives must be stated clearly and in terms of learner performance! Each objective should tell who is to do what, when and how! Several examples of performance objectives appear beginning on page 51 and through page 53 in Part I of this book. These may be used as is or adapted as desired. You will need to specify many more of your own, however, to complete this phase of curriculum development. A worksheet which might facilitate the process of writing the objectives appears on the following page.

It should be kept in mind that a curriculum is a set of suggested alternatives for teaching, not a detailed instructional plan. Therefore, the objectives written at this level should be comprehensive enough to allow the individual teacher to pick and choose among alternatives, and to become more specific and detailed, if necessary.

TIP

Curriculum development literature suggests that the process should involve many people and should especially include all who will use the resulting curriculum.

Technology Curriculum Objectives

for

Grade_____School_____District_____

TOPIC: Hardware, Software, Programming, Social Impact, Other (Circle)

Sub-Topic (if any):_____

Objective(s):

1._____ _

_____

2._____ _

_____

3._____ _

_____

4._____ _

_____

5._____ _

_____

6._____ _

_____

7._____ _

_____

Evaluation Devices

As soon as the objectives are defined, the evaluation techniques and devices for measuring student learning should be developed. Wherever possible, of course, these should be performance based evaluation criteria, in keeping with the performance based objectives. Again, these suggestions for evaluating student learning should provide alternatives for final selection by individual teachers. In order to provide many alternatives, the suggestions are not always fully developed as evaluation instruments at this point, but are examples of instruments only.

Evaluation is mentioned here because of its importance in the curriculum. Experience has shown that if the development of the evaluation component is delayed until the end of the process, it often suffers from lack of adequate attention. Therefore, though it is often the last component used in actual teaching, early development has been recommended over and over by many experts.

There should be evaluation criteria for every objective, but one way to reduce the task of writing evaluation is to group the objectives according to the type of performance specified in the objectives. To do this, alternative schemes already exist which may be appropriate. The objectives may be classified according to the Taxonomy of Educational Objectives (Bloom et al. 1956; Krathwahl et al. 1964) as follows:

Cognitive Domain   **Affective Domain**
Knowledge   Receiving
Comprehension   Responding
Application   Valuing
Analysis   Organization
Synthesis   Characterization
Evaluation

By classifying the objectives, a single instrument can be used to measure attainment of objectives in a single category, perhaps as broad as all cognitive objectives or, if more desirable, all knowledge objectives, comprehension objectives, etc. In the cognitive domain only the

categories offered by Gagné (1974) may be even more useful for developing evaluation procedures. These include:
Discrimination

> Concrete Concepts
> Defined Concept
> Rule
> Higher Order Rule
> Cognitive Strategies
> Attitudes
> Motor Skills

Activities

Instructional activities should be included in the curriculum plan for each major goal, objective, or topic. For teaching about hardware, there should be ready access to appropriate equipment and alternative problems or simulated activities to permit considerable hands-on opportunities for the learners. To teach about software, the activities must involve the use of software, plus the original design—if not programming—of original applications. Programming, likewise, requires actual doing, and if the problem for which the programmer is seeking a solution is an important one to the programmer, more effort will likely be given to solving the problem and completing the program. Finally, the social impact topic requires activities which make very clear to the learners some of the vast effects technology has had upon their lives in recent years.

Keep in mind as you develop the curriculum activities that there should be several types of activities for each topic. These alternatives may or may not be included in the curriculum, but eventually they will need to be present when the curriculum is actually implemented. Activities for each topic should include those that:

> Set the stage and motivate the learners;

> Relate to prior learning for building upon previous skills and knowledge;

> Provide opportunity for actual performance;

Provide opportunity for practice and feedback;

Provide for transfer to other performance.

Curriculum literature (Taba 1962) has often called for three types of activities for these purposes: Introductory, Developmental, and Culminating. A framework could be established that would enable curriculum developers to include all of these three types of activities for each objective in the curriculum. An example of a worksheet which might be used appears below.

Worksheet for Planning Activities for Educational Technology Curriculum

	Motivate	Recall	Objectives	Stimulus	Feedback
Hardware					
1.					
2.					
3.					
Software					
1.					
2.					
3.					
Programming					
1.					
2.					
3.					
Social Impact					
1.					
2.					
3.					

Materials

Finally, for the instructional materials to be included in the curriculum. There will, of course, need to be manuals or books for the hardware written for various grade levels, ample software and good documentation (manuals or on the disk itself) to facilitate effective use, books on programming and a supply of programming reference manulas, written sheets with simulated problems to which learners can provide programming solutions, and literature about the history and impact of technology on the individual, the home, the neighborhood, the state, the nation, and the world. There will also be an abundance of current periodical literature dealing with this last topic in magazines and newspapers.

To accomplish the task of selecting appropriate materials, it might be most appropriate to appoint committees with representatives from all grade levels to review the extensive collection of literature now available. One strategy which has been successfully used in many schools is to sponsor a "Computer Fair" to which vendors and publishers alike are invited to come and share their products. Short of this, sending a few representatives to national conferences, such as those listed in Part III, might suffice. At any rate, the materials selection is a major undertaking that will require considerable attention and care.

Summary

This chapter has presented a plan for developing a technology curriculum for use in the schools. The plan proposed includes the objectives, activities, materials, and evaluation devices needed for any curriculum. This is an important part of the total technology plan for any school and should receive a great deal of attention.

References

Bloom, B. S., et al. *The Taxonomy of Educational Objectives, Cognitive Domain*. New York: David McKay Company, Inc., 1956.

Gagné, Robert M. *Essentials of Learning for Instruction*. Hinsdale, Ill.: Dryden Press, 1974.

Krathwahl, David, et al. *The Taxonomy of Educational Objectives, Affective Domain*. New York: David McKay Company, Inc., 1964.

Mager, Robert F. and Pipe, Peter. *Analyzing Performance Problems*. Belmont, Cal.: Fearon Publishers, 1970.

Taba, Hilda. *Curriculum Development, Theory and Practice*. New York: Harcourt, Brace, & World, Inc., 1962.

Tyler, Ralph. *Basic Principles of Curriculum and Instruction*. Chicago: University of Chicago Press, 1949.

Index

Selected Bibliography for Suggested Reading

Ahl, David. *Basic Games*. Morristown, N.J.: Creative Computing Press, 1976.

Ahl, David. *More Basic Computer Games*. Morristown, N . J.: Creative Computing Press, 1977.

American School Board Journal, "The Electronic School" 175no.9(Sept. 1988):A1-A32

Anderson, Ronald E. "Computer Simulation Games, Exemplars." In *The Guide to Simulations/Games for Education and Training*. 4th ed. Edited by R. E. Horn and A. Cleves. Beverly Hills: Sage Publications, 1980.

Anderson, R. E., Hansen, Thomas, Johnson, David C., and Klassen, D. "Instructional Computing: Acceptance and Rejection." *Sociology of Work and Occupations* 6 (1979): 227-250.

Bailey, H. Whitney. "The Computer Interactive Videodisc." *Filmmakers Monthly,* November 1980, 11-28.

Beck, J. J., Jr. Computer Literacy for Elementary and Secondary Teachers. Paper presented at the annual meeting of the Texas Association for Supervision and Curriculum Development, Houston, April 1980.

Bejar, Issac I. "Videodiscs in Education: Integrating the Computer and Communications Technologies." *Byte* (June 1982):78-104.

Billings, Karen, and Moursund, David. *Are You Computer Literate?* Forest Grove, Ore.: Dilithium Press, 1979.

Boyd, Gary. "The Impact of Society on Educational Technology." *British Journal of Educational Technology* 19no.2(May 1988):16-18.

Bork, A. "Computers in Education Today-and Some Possible Futures." *Phi Delta Kappan,* December 1984, 239-243.

Bork, A. *Personal Computers for Education.* New York: Harper & Row Publishers, 1985.

Brisson, D. "Making the Grade at Keene High School." *Microcomputing*(June 1980):108-110.

Caissey, G. A. "Evaluating Educational Software: A Practitioner's Guide." *Phi Delta Kappan* (December 1984):249-250.

Center for Social Organization of Schools. *School Uses of Microcomputers.* Baltimore: Johns Hopkins University.

Chambers, J. A. , and Sprecher, J. W. "Computer Assisted Instruction: Current Thinking and Critical Issues." *Communications of Association for Computing Machinery* (June 1980):332-342.

Clement, Frank. "Oh, Dad, Poor Dad — Mom's Bought the Wrong Videodisc and I'm Sad." *Instructional Innovator* (February 1981):13.

Commission on Instructional Technology. *To Improve Learning.* Washington: US Government Printing Office, 1970.

Covvey, Dominic, and McAlister, Neil Harding. *Computer Consciousness: Surviving the Automated 80s.* Reading, Mass.: Addison-Wesley Publishing Company, Inc., 1980.

Damarin, Suzanne K. "Re-thinking Equity: An Imperative for Educational Computing." *The Computing Teacher* 16no.7(April 1989):16-18.

Daynes, Rod. "The Videodisc Interfacing Primer." *Byte* (June 1982):48-59.

Dearborn, Donald E. "Computer Literacy." *Educational Leadership* (September 1983):32-34.

Denee, Jean. "Interactive Videodiscs: A New Instructional Technology." *Business Education Forum* 42no.6(March 1988):3-5.

D'Ignazio, Fred. "Bringing the 1990's to the Classroom of Today." *Phi Delta Kappan* 70no.1(Sept. 1988):26-27.

Downing, Bruce. "More on Planning for Computers in Education." *Commodore Magazine* (June/July 1982):27-28.

Dwyer, Thomas, and Critchfield, Margot. *BASIC and the Personal Computer.* Reading, Mass.: Addison-Wesley Publishing Company, Inc., 1978.

Edwards, Judith B.; Ellis, Antoinette; Richardson, Duane; Holznagel, Donald; and Kassen, Daniel. *Computer Applications in Instruction: A Teacher's Guide to Selection and Use.* Hanover, N. H.: TSC/ Houghton Mifflin Company, 1978.

Edwards, Carol. "Project MiCRO." *The Computing Teacher* 16no.5(February 1989):11-13.

Eisele, James E. *Computer Assisted Planning of Curriculum and Instruction.* Englewood Cliffs: Educational Technology Publications, 1971.

Etherington, John. "Producing for Videodiscs: Strange New World." *E & ITV* (March 1981):37.

Floyd, Steve, and Floyd, Beth. *Handbook of Interactive Video.* White Plains, N. Y.: Knowledge Industry Publications, Inc., 1982.

Fredericks, A. "Computer Workshops That Don't Fail." *Electronic Education* 4 (1984): 21-22.

Freyd, Pamela. "What Educators Really Want in Software Design." *Media and Methods* (Mar/Apr 1989):44-47.

Gleason, G. T. "Microcomputers in Education: The State of the Art." *Educational Technology* (1981):7-18.

Goodlad, John I. "Essay One: The Curriculum." in *Rational Planning of Curriculum and Instruction*. Washington: National Education Association, 1967.

Grady, M. Tim, and Poirot, James L. *Teacher Competence: What is Needed: Computers in Curriculum and Instruction*. Alexandria, Va.: Association for Supervision and Curriculum Development, 1983.

Hargon, Carol, and Hunter, Beverly. *Instructional Computing . . . Ten Case Studies*. Alexandria, Va.: Human Resources Research Organization, 1974.

Harper, D. O., and Stewart, J. H. Teacher Education. In *Run: Computer Education*, 2nd ed. Edited by D. O. Harper and J. H. Stewart. Monterey, Cal.: Brooks/Cole Publishing Company, 1986.

Harte, David V. "The Search for 21st Century Mindware." *Community, Technical and Junior College Journal* 58no.2(Oct,-Nov. 1987):50-53.

Hawley, John F. and Jane Y. Murdock. "Technology and Students With Handicaps." *Contemporary Educational Psychology* 12no.3(July 1987):212-221.

Heck, William P.; Johnson, Jerry; and Kansky, Robert J. *Guidelines for Evaluating Computerized Instructional Materials*. Reston, Va.: National Council of Teachers of Mathematics, 1981

Holden, Constance. "Computers Make Slow Progress in Class." *Science* 244no.26(May 1989):906-909.

Hunter, Beverly. *My Students Use Computers*. Reston, Va.: Reston Publishing Company, Inc., 1984.

Jirka, Charles C. and Sharon E. Smaldino. "Computer Assisted Instruction." *Middle School Journal* 20no.4(March 1989)26-28.

Johnson, D., Anderson, R. E., Hansen, T. P., and Klassen, D. L. "Computer Literacy: What is It?" *Mathematics Teacher* 73no. 2(1980):91-96.

Judd, Wallace. "A Teacher's Place in the Computer Curriculum." *Phi Delta Kappan* (October 1983):120-122.

Kindleberger, Charles P. "Whither the Interactive Videodisc?" *E-ITV,* (October 1982):60-65.

Kingman, James. "Designing Good Educational Software." *Creative Computing* 7no.1(October 1981): 72, 74, 76, 78, 80-81.

Kleiman, Glenn; Humphrey, Mary M.; and Van Buskirk, Trudy. "Evaluating Educational Software." *Creative Computing* 7no.10 (October 1981): 84, 86, 88, 90.

Knirk, Frederick G., and Gustafson, Kent L. *Instructional Technology.* New York: Holt, Rinehart, and Winston, Inc., 1986.

Komoski, P. K. "Educational Computing: The Burden of Insuring Quality." *Phi Delta Kappan* (December 1984):244-248.

LaPointe, Archie and Michael Martinez. "Aims, Equity and Access in Computer Education." *Phi Delta Kappan* 70no.1(Sept. 1988):59-61.

Lee, Chris. "Adding the New Technology to Your Training Repertoire." *Training* (April 1982):18-26.

Lee, H. C. "Ten Tips for Finding Good Reading Software." *Computers, Reading, and Language Arts* 2(1984):26-27.

Ley, Kathryn L. "CD ROM: Searching With Speed." *Media and Methods* (March/April 1989).

Lippman, A. "Movie Maps: An Application of the Optical Videodisc to Computer Graphics." SIGGRAPH '80 Conference Proceedings. *Computer Graphics* 14 (July 1980): 32-42.

Lockheed, M.; Nielson, A.; and Stone, M. Sex Differences in Microcomputer Literacy. In *Proceedings of the National Educational Computer Conference.* Baltimore, Minn.,: NECC, 1983.

Loop, Liza, and Christenson, Paul. *Exploring the Microcomputer Learning Environment.* Independent Research Project Report No. 5. San

Francisco: Far West Laboratory for Educational Research and Development, 1980.

Luehrmann, Arthur; Peckman, Herbert; and Ramirez, Martha. *A First Course in Computing*. New York: McGraw-Hill Book Company, 1982.

Malone, Linda, and Johnson, Jerry. *BASIC Discoveries*. Palo Alto, Calif.: Creative Publications, 1981.

Malone, Thomas, W. *What Makes Things Fun to Learn?* Palo Alto, Calif.: Xerox Palo Alto Research Center, 1980.

Melmed, Arthur. "The Technology of Education Problem and Opportunity." *Technological Horizons in Education* 14no.2(Sept. 1986):77-81.

Moss, James R. "Utah: A Case Study." *Phi Delta Kappan* 70no,1(Sept. 1988):25-26.

Mowe, Richard. *The Academic Apple*. Reston, Va.: Reston Publishing Company, Inc., 1983.

Nugent, Ron. *An Overview of Videodisc Technology*. Lincoln, Neb.: Videodisc Design/Production Group KUON-TV/University of Nebraska-Lincoln, October 1980.

Olds, Henry; Schwarz, Judah; and Willie, Nancy. *People and Computers: Who Teaches Whom?* Newton, Mass.: Educational Development Center, Inc., 1980.

Olivas, Jerry. "Yes, You Can Run the Front Office on a Microcomputer System." *Classroom Computer Learning* 8no.6(march 1989):46-49.

Pantiel, M., and Peterson, B. Strategies of Teacher Training. In *Kids, Teachers, and Computers*. Edited by Mindy Pantiel and B. Peterson. Englewood Cliffs, N. J.: Prentice Hall, 1984.

Papert, Seymour; Abelson, Harold; diSessa, Andrea; Watt, Daniel; and Weir, Sylvia. *The Final Report of the Brookline LOGO Project: As-*

sessment and Documentation of a Children's Computer Laboratory. MIT LOGO Memo 53 and 54. Cambridge, Mass.: MIT LOGO Group,1980.

Perelman, Lewis. "Restructuring the System." *Phi Delta Kappan* 70no.1 (Sept. 1988):20-24.

Performance & Instruction Journal 22, no. 9 (November 1983). Entire issue devoted to interactive video.

Peter, Hal, and Johnson, James. *Author's Guide: Design Development Style Packaging Review.* Iowa City, Ia.: Conduit, 1978.

Preston, S. M., and Lee, J. F. *Educational Technology Local Planning Guide.* Atlanta, Ga.: Georgia Department of Education, 1985.

Roberts, Nancy. "Introducing Computer Simulations into the High Schools: An Applied Mathematics Curriculum." *Mathematics Teacher* 74no.1(November 1981):647-652.

Rosen, Marion. "LEGO Meets LOGO." *Classroom Computer Learning* 8no.7(April 1988):50-51.

Sandoval, H. F. Teacher Training in Computer Skills. *Educational Technology* 24 , no. 10 (1984), 29-31.

Sigel, Efrem, et al. *Video Discs: The Technology, the Applications and the Future.* White Plains, N. Y.: Knowledge Industry Publications, Inc., 1980.

Thomas, D. B., and McClain, D. H. "Selecting Microcomputers for the Classroom."*AEDS Journal* 12(Fall 1979):55-68.

Thomas, James L., ed. *Microcomputers in the Schools.* Phoenix, Ariz.: The Oryx Press, 1981.

Turner, Judith Axler. "Teacher Training Colleges' Slow Move to Computers Blamed for Schools' Lag in Integrating Technology." *Chronicle of Higher Education* 35no.45(July 19, 1989):A9-A11.

Video Systems. Overland Park, Kan.: Intertec Publishing Corp., monthly.

Videography. New York: United Business Publications, Inc., monthly.

Videodisc Design/Production Group News. Lincoln, Neb.: Nebraska ETV Network/University of Nebraska-Lincoln, monthly

Videodisc/Videotex. Westport, Conn.: Meckler Publishing, monthly.

Watt, Daniel. "A Comparison of the Problem Solving Styles of Two Children Learning LOGO: A Computer Language for Children." Proceedings of the National Educational Computing Conference, 1979, University of Iowa. Reprinted in *Creative Computing* 5no.12 (December 1979).

Wilderquist, Kristine. "Course Design for Training Secondary Teachers to Develop Interactive Videodisc Courseware." *Technological Horizons in Education* 14no.6(February 1987):68-72.

Willis, Jerry. *Peanut Butter and Jelly Guide to Computers.* Beaverton, Ore.: Dilithium Press, 1978.

Willis, Jerry, and Donley, William, Jr. *Nailing Jelly to a Tree.* Beaverton, Ore.: Dilithium Press, 1981.

Winslow, Ken. "Videodisc Systems—A Retrospective." *E & ITV*, (March 1981):38-39.

Part III

Glossary

Address: a variable name that designates a location where information is stored in a memory device

Algorithm: a step-by-step solution to a problem

ASCIE: a uniform set of binary codes representing numbers, symbols, and letters; acronym for American Standard Code for Information Exchange

BASIC: a computer programming language which uses English words and mathematical symbols; acronym for Beginners All-Purpose Symbolic Instruction Code

Baud: rate of transfer of data which is stated in bits per second

Binary Code: a code which uses two symbols, 1 and 0, to represent data.

Bus: electrical lines which connect components of a computer; data are transmitted through these lines

Byte: a unit of information which usually consists of one character composed of eight bits

CAI: computer assisted instruction; usually consists of a program which is loaded into a computer for use of individuals or groups

Character: numbers, letters, and symbols which make up information sets; each character is usually made of one byte of information

Computer literacy: knowledge of the functions and instructional applications of computers, peripherals, and software

Courseware: instructional software written in a programming language such as BASIC or PILOT

CPU: the brain of the computer which correlates all functions of the computer; acronym for Central Processing Unit

CRT: tube which produces an image on a television screen and is used to display text and graphics produced by a computer; acronym for Cathode Ray Tube

Cursor: a movable image on the CRT which indicates where the next character will appear

Data: information put into and taken from a computer

Debug: to locate and delete errors in a computer program

Dialog: a complex, little used type of CAI in which students submit data or questions to the computer which replies with correct answers and additional information

Disc: standard use of this spelling refers to videodisc storage devices

Disk (diskette): a mass storage device which stores and retrieves information at a high rate of speed; can be flexible (floppy disk) or rigid (hard disk)

Dot matrix: a technique which uses dots to create characters; a minimal 5 X 7 array will create alphanumeric characters while 7 X 9 or other arrays will create letters and underlining

Duplex: an interface which permits communication between computers and peripheral devices

EPROM: long term memory which can be erased and rewritten; acronym for Erasable Programmable Read Only Memory

File: a set of related data

Floppy disk: a flexible mass data storage device (see **disk**)

Firmware: programs stored in ROM which do not need to be loaded from a storage device

Floating point BASIC: a BASIC programming language which can handle mathematical equations and words or strings of non-numeric data

GIGO: garbage in, garbage out; input errors will result in output errors

Graphics: a computer's capability to produce drawings, graphs, charts, and so on, on a monitor or printer

Graphic subroutine: a section of a program which performs specific graphic functions; can substitute graphics for words

Hardware: equipment which composes a computer system

High-level language: a computer language which consists of words, arithmetic, and common mathematical symbols; each instruction represents a variety of computer operations

Input: information going into a computer or peripheral; such information may also be output of another part of the computer system

Interface: a device which connects a computer to a peripheral such as a printer

I/O: input/output of information

K or Kilo: symbol for 1,000; in computer language; 1 K represents 2 to the tenth power, or 1024

Machine language: language, usually consisting of series of binary numbers or hexidecimal numbers, which can be read by a computer

Memory: high speed electronic parts of a computer which store information in ROM or RAM

Modem: an interface which allows computers to send and receive electronic signals over telecommunication lines or satellites; acronym for modulator-demodulator

Output: data coming out of a computer

Peripheral device: hardware, such as printers and disc drives, linked to a computer through an interface

PILOT : a programming language which uses conversation and interaction techniques; developed by Dr. John Starkweather

PROM: unalterable data permanently stored in RAM; acronym for Programmable Read Only Memory

RAM: alterable working memory of the computer; acronym for Random Access Memory

REM: a REMark statement in a computer program; explains part of the program and does not have to be put into the computer's memory

ROM: similar to PROM but is installed by the computer's manufacturer; acronym for Read Only Memory

Software: programs and documentation which make a computer function

Tutorial: a type of CAI which uses programmed instruction

Terminal: a peripheral which is made up of a CRT or printer, a keyboard, and sometimes a disk device

Appendices

Needs Assessment Resourses

1. Resource list of Needs Assessment tools.

2. Who Needs Training for Which Competencies?

3. Survey of Supervisor's Needs for Training in the Use of Educational Technology.

4. Needs Assessment.

5. Needs Assessment Tools: Checklist of Steps.

Resource List of Needs Assessment Tools

Needs Assessment Publications and Publishers of Models

Alameda County Needs Assessment Model (ACNAM). Office of the Alameda County Superintendent of Schools, 685 A Street, Hayward, CA 94541.*

Atlanta Assessment Project. Instructional Services Center, 2930 Forrest Hill Dr., SE, Atlanta, Georgia 30315.

Batelle's Surveys. Center for Improved Education, Batelle Memorial Institute, 505 King Avenue, Columbus, Ohio 43201

CSE/Elementary Evaluation Kit: Needs Assessment. Allyn and Bacon, Inc., Longwood Division, 470 Atlantic Avenue, Boston, Massachusetts 02210.

Dallas Model. Dallas Independent School District, 3700 Ross Avenue, Dallas, Texas 75204.

Florida Needs Assessment Development Project. Florida State Department of Education, Tallahassee, Florida 32301.

"Institutional Goals Inventory (IGI)." Educational Testing Service, College and University Programs, P.O. Box 3813, Princeton, New Jersey 08540.

Phi Delta Kappa Model. Phi Delta Kappa, Commision on Educational Planning, P.O. Box 789, Bloomington, IN 47401.

Pupil Perceived Needs Assessment Package. Research for Better Schools, Inc., 1700 Market Street, Philadelphia, PA 19103.

Quality Education Program Study (QEPS). Office of the Bucks County Superintendent of Schools, Doylestown, PA 18901.

"Research and Development Utilization Project." Georgia State Department of Education, 1862 Twin Towers East, Atlanta, Georgia 30334.

Rookey, T. Jerome. Needs Assessment Model: East Stroudsburg State College, Monroe County, PA, May, 1975.

South Carolina Needs Assessment Model. Office of Planning and Evaluation, South Carolina Department of Education, 608 Rutledge Building, Columbia, South Carolina 29210.

Managing Needs Assessment

Bishop, Leslee J. "Casual Analysis Re Instructional Needs." University of Georgia Department of Curriculum and Supervision, Athens, GA 30602.

Dick, Walter and Lou M. Carey. "Needs Assessment and Instructional Design." Florida State University, Tallahassee, FL

English, Fenwick W. and Roger A. Kaufman. Needs Assessment: A Focus for Curriculum Development. Washington, D.C.: Association for Supervision and Curriculum Development.

Hoenes, Ronald L., N. Kemp Mabry, and John M. Morris. District/School Perceived Needs Assessment Package. Georgia Southern College, Statesboro, Georgia 30458 1976.

Needs Assessment in Education: A Planning Handbook for School Districts. State of New Jersey, Department of Education, Division of Research, Planning and Evaluation, 225 West State Street, Trenton, NJ 08625, February, 1976.

Nix, Jack P. "Needs Assessment Package." Georgia State Department of Education, Division of Program and Staff Development, Office of Instructional Services, Atlanta, Georgia 30334.

"Pupil Perceived Needs Assessment Package." Research for Better Schools, Inc., 1700 Market Street Philadelphia, PA 19103.

"We the People..." School Board of Brevard County, 3205 South Washington Avenue, Titusville, FL 32780.

Wentling, Tim L. and Len Albright. Administrator's Manual for the Identification and Assessment System. Bureau of Educational Research, University of Illinois at Urbana-Champaign.

Management System: Needs Assessment Program Worksheets and Handouts. Education Improvement Center-South, Woodbury-Glassboro Road, Pitman, NJ 08071. (609-589-3410)

From *Educational Technology: Local Planning Guide* by Stephen Foster and Jane Lee. Reprinted by permission.

Who Needs Training for Which Competencies?

The next step is to ascertain which staff members need training for which competencies. This can be determined through a short self-report which can be distributed to all staff. A partial example of such an inventory follow.

Computing Skills Inventory

Name _____   Grade _____

School _____ Subject _____

In an effort to tailor staff development for improving our use of educational technology, the planners would like assistance in determining what should be included in the training program. Would you please help by indicating your strengths and where you feel additional help is needed in this vital area.

Competency	Skill Level					Need More?	
	High	**Medium**		**Low**		**Yes**	**No**
To identify appropriate hardware.	5	4	3	2	1		
To maintain hardware.	5	4	3	2	1		
To operate equipment.	5	4	3	2	1		
To select software.	5	4	3	2	1		
To maintain software.	5	4	3	2	1		
To use applications.	5	4	3	2	1		
To define a problem.	5	4	3	2	1		
To design a solution.	5	4	3	2	1		
To write a program.	5	4	3	2	1		
To understand impact of technology on society	5	4	3	2	1		

Eisele, UGA

Survey of Supervisor's Needs for Training in the Use of Educational Technology

Directions: Following is a list of topics pertaining to the use of technology, especially microcomputers, in education. In order to determine content appropriate for teaching school supervisors about educational technology, you are to rate each topic for its importance to the job of a school supervisor. Please use the following scale in rating each item:

1 = not relevant
2 = relevant but not really important to the job
3 = important for job performance
4 = very important but not essential for job performance
5 = essential to successful job performance

1. History of computing.	1	2	3	4	5
2. Influence of computers on society.	1	2	3	4	5
3. Future developments in microcomputers.	1	2	3	4	5
4. How computers work – their operations.	1	2	3	4	5
5. Components of computer systems.	1	2	3	4	5
6. Programming in a computer language.	1	2	3	4	5
7. Creation of computer language.	1	2	3	4	5
8. Using word processing applications.	1	2	3	4	5
9. Using database applications.	1	2	3	4	5
10. Using educational applications.	1	2	3	4	5
11. Using spread sheet applications	1	2	3	4	5
12. Evaluating microcomputer software.	1	2	3	4	5
13. Teaching computer topics to pupils.	1	2	3	4	5
14. Designing instructional applications.	1	2	3	4	5
15. Altering or fixing ready-made programs.	1	2	3	4	5
16. Limitations of computers.	1	2	3	4	5
17. Using statistical applications.	1	2	3	4	5
18. Using computers to teach problem solving.	1	2	3	4	5
19. Using administrative applications.	1	2	3	4	5
20. Planning for utilization of technology.	1	2	3	4	5
21. Evaluating technology programs in schools.	1	2	3	4	5
22. Sources of educational applications.	1	2	3	4	5
23. Research on computer use in education.	1	2	3	4	5
24. Selecting and acquiring hardware.	1	2	3	4	5
25. Using instructional support applications.	1	2	3	4	5
26. Other topics (please list)	1	2	3	4	5
	1	2	3	4	5

Needs Assessment*

Instructional Question:	**Media Selection Question:**	**Design Question:**
What student performance gaps exist?	What functions need to be performed in order to close the performance gap?	What alternatives are available to perform the needed functions given existing constraints?
Source of info:	**Source of info:**	**Source of info:**
Needs Assessment	Instructional Design Literature	Media selection Models
Output:	**Output:**	**Output:**
Needs statement	List of functions to be performed	Best alternative means for closing the gaps.

*From Salisbury, David F. Needs Assessment, Instructional Design, and the Use of Microcomputers for Instruction. *1984 Proceedings of the Association for the Development of Computer Based Instructional Systems.* Philadelphia: The Association, 1984. p. 57.

Needs Assessment Tools: Checklist of Steps

This checklist describes what to do to conduct a system-wide needs assessment. The process recommended here consists of six basic steps. The checklist can be used in several ways. It has been designed in what experience has shown to be a logical, sequential order for use in a cookbook fashion by a project coordinator or steering committee. As with a recipe, any step or ingredient which is left out will affect the quality of the product. A second, less strict, application is to use the checklist as a directory, that is, as a source of recommendations which can be altered according to local circumstances. This checklist is also ideal as a tool for review to be sure that the planners have successfully completed each task, and to verify that any which have been left out were left out by rational choice rather than through an oversight. The sequence is varied or the elements changed, be sure to do so only after careful consideration.

Step 1 Initiate the needs assessment process

This step entails gearing up for the needs assessment: selecting needs assessment committee members, orienting them and making tentative plans.

Task 1 Establish a Needs Assessment Committee
      Select a coordinator
      Identify a resource person
      Outline required committee with cross sectional representation

Task 2 Orient the Committee to the Overall Needs Assessment Process
      Brief committee members on strategies, recommendations
      Identify current resources and constraints

Task 3 Make Tentative Plans
      Review specific needs assessment components
      Determine desired comprehensiveness of the local plan
      Determine individual committee member responsibilities
      Set tentative timelines

Step 2 Conduct perceived needs assessment

School publics are surveyed to determine what they view as the top school needs. It is recommended that the publics surveyed include administrators, teachers, and students, and the approximately five top needs of each group be identified and then merged into one list.

Task 1 Review/ Finalize the Perceived Needs Assessment Process
Specify target individuals or sample sizes
Finalize instruments
Detail administration procedures
Define points to be made to each target group
Finalize data analysis mechanics

Task 2 Conduct the Perceived Needs Assessments
Conduct school administration assessment
Conduct teacher/school staff assessment
Conduct a student assessment

Task 3 Identify Sets of Top Needs
Score the instruments
Determine top needs by group
Merge into one cross system list

Step 3 Verify perceived needs by objective means

The aim of Step 3 is the verification by objective means each of the top perceived needs to determine that a major problem, limitation, or discrepency does exsist. That is, do test data, structured observations, interview data or other means (existing or new) bear out the identified needs? Thus, the list is further delineated.

Task 1 Plan for Verification
Orient committee on possible verification tools
Select objective means to verify each need (existing or new)
Plan for administration (procedures, timeline)

Task 2 Validate the Perceived Needs
      Collect/compile existing or new data
      Analyze all data
      Compare perceived needs with analysis of objective measures
      Finalize the cross system perceived needs list

Step 4 Determine System-wide need priorities

One cross-system survey instrument is developed and administered during Step 4. A discrepency-type instrument is suggested for surveying everyone's perception of:(1) the importance of addressing a need and (2) the degree to which this need has been met to date. From these perceptions, needs can be rank ordered, resulting in a system-wide list of priority needs.

Task 1 Organize for a System-wide Ranking of Needs
      Review the plan for determining system-wide priorities
      Develop one cross-system survey instrument
      Determine groups to respond/sample sizes
      Determine procedures for ranking resulting needs
      Specify administrative mechanics

Task 2 Conduct the Assessment
      Administer the instrument (distribute/collect)
      Score the instruments

Task 3 Place Cross-System Needs in Priority Order
      Rank order the needs
      Compile priority list of cross-system needs

Step 5 Choose need to be addressed by improvement efforts

Step 5 involves deciding which of the system-wide needs is to be the focus of improvement. It is recommended that one (or possibly two if they are closely related) be identified by weighing what is most desirable to address and what resources are available. Obtaining school system approval and communicating undertakings to the educational public are also parts of the step.

Task 1 Determine Which Need is to be Improved
>> Estimate the resources required to tackle each need
>> Select needs to address

Task 2 Obtain School System Approval
>> Obtain central administrative approval
>> Obtain school board approval

Task 3 Communicate Findings/Undertakings to the Public
>> Decide on points to be made to various publics/presentation modes
>> Present information within the system (faculty, students)
>> Communicate information to parents/community

Step 6 Conduct a causal analysis of the need to be improved

This step requires a look at factors which might have caused the identified need. Six factors are recommended for analysis in relation to the need: students, teachers, curriculum, resources, management and the community. The causal analysis study is to delimit or redefine the need with respect to possible causal influences. A master list of causes is generated and ranked, and a report published.

Task 1 Organize to Conduct the Causal Analysis
>> Review the process
>> Assemble/orient representatives from the need area(s) affected
>> Determine additional support required
>> Set timelines, responsibilities

Task 2 Analyze the Need in Relation to Six Causal Areas
>> Decide which are the Six Causal Areas to investigate
>> Describe desired conditions in each area
>> Examine interrelationships across six areas
>> Select analysis tools or techniques for data collection
>> Collect and analyze data

Task 3 Place Causal Factors in Priority Order
        Generate a list of primary causal factors
        Decide which have the greatest impact on the system
        Place the Causal factors in priority order
        Choose final areas to attack through an improvement effort

Task 4 Evaluate Your Needs Assessment Program Using "Needs Assessment: Checklist of Steps"

Task 5 Develop a Report of Causal Factors
        Submit report to Central Administration and Board for
            Approval
        Communicate report to educational community and public

From *Educational Technology: Local Planning Guide* by Stephen Preston and Jane Lee, Reprinted by permission.

Planning and Management Resources

1. Computer Acquisition Contracts.

2. Networking for Microcomputer Management.

3. Stage Six - Checklist for Organizing and Implementing.

Computer Acquisition Contracts

by Patricia A. Hollander

When a computer malfunctions, the results can be ruinous. Here's an actual description of a relatively small, but wayward typesetting computer: "The RAM board was not functional; the keyboard locked up; the viewing screen blanked out or information shown on the screen did not transfer to the photo, unit produced crooked lines, bouncy type, spontaneous capitalization, and shadow images. The disk drive alignment malfunctioned, erasing information recorded onto the floppy disks." The owners of the computer described their experience as "...devastating...Production delays, poor quality output and the inability to retrieve stored data caused plaintiffs to lose customers and profits, professional prestige, and to expend funds on nonproductive employee labor."

But they were fortunate - their computer acquisition contract had been drawn carefully to provide protection for just such a contingency. They sued the vendor for damages based on the value of the data stored in the computer, lost profits, employee's wages, and purchase price of the machine. A court found the vendor not only breached implied and express warranties but also negligently misrepresented the capability, suitability, reliability, serviceability, and profitability of the computer. Awarded damages amounted to $117,797.55. (Barnard v. Compugraphic Corporation, 667P.2d 1171, Wash.App. 1983).

Acquisition Process Guidelines. Whether you plan to acquire a single computer or a complex system, take time to follow some basic guidelines:

> Know exactly what you expect the computer to do, and write those expectations into the contract.
>
> Get independent expert advice.
>
> Seek software first, hardware second.
>
> Ask to see the recommended computer in operation.
>
> Talk to people using it.

Ask about compatibility, updating, and maintenance.

Ask about training personnel.

Try to get all terms and conditions of the agreement in writing.

When writing the sales contract begin by incorporating into it not only product expectations but also which components the vendor has recommended to meet those expectations. Next, describe and specify software and hardware components unit by unit to find out if the vendor warrants component compatibility for both basic and peripheral equipment.

The checklist below covers some typical terms and conditions to consider in a computer acquisition contract. It is abbreviated in content and not meant to be all inclusive, but is intended to assist readers in developing lists relative to their own situations.

1. Is the contract written in terms of the result expected by the user of the system (e.g. corporate-level recordkeeping, computer-assisted manufacturing, payroll processing, registration of students)?

2. Are hardware and software specified unit by unit?

3. Does the contract incorporate detailed specifications regarding computer system performance, such as:

> a. specific functions the supplier says will be done (e.g. providing numerical and geographical inventory data, printing tabular reports)

> b. what the supplier will do regarding matters such as:
> 1. site preparation

> 2. date and method of delivery-penalties for delay

> 3. installation

> 4. compatibility of components

> 5. documentation

      6. providing personnel

      7. training personnel

      8. testing

      9. guarantees of reliability

      10. security of equipment

      11. confidentiality of user's data

      12. maintenance

      13. modifications

  c. what the user will do regarding
      1. providing clean power

      2. providing a proper environment

      3. providing qualified staff

      4. accepting delivery after testing

4. Financial Matters

  a. are rental, purchase, timesharing, or service bureau terms clear, accurate, and mutually understood?

  b. what discounts apply?

  c. what tax issues should be discussed?

  d. what are the penalties for partial or non-performance?

  e. what backups are there for downtime?

5. Insurance

   a. what coverage is there for damage to, or inquiry resulting from, equipment or personnel?

   b. what coverage protects the loss of business?

From *Educom Bulletin*, Summer 1985 by Patricia A. Holland. Reprinted by permission of author.

Networking For Microcomputer Management

Kenneth Forman, Community School District 27

Carl Steinhoff, New York University

A network of several microcomputers connected to a common hard disk storage system provides several administrative functions for effective management.

Community School District 27 is one of the 32 public school districts within the City of New York with approximately 27,000 pupils in grades K-9 and 1,400 employees. Early in 1980, we began to investigate the feasibility of using computers for evaluative and management purposes. This investigation was a collaborative effort with our evaluation consultant, New York University, under the leadership of Dr. Carl Steinhoff. We determined that microcomputers would cost effectively manage all the various applications we desired to implement for fiscal, information and evaluative reporting.

Several microcomputer systems were investigated including: Apple, Atari, Bell and Howell, Commodore/Pet, Radio Shack, etc. Upon receiving the literature, we came upon the successful experiences of MECC (Minnesota Educational Computing Consortium) with Apple microcomputers. The Apple microcomputer offered numerous applications in the areas of business, financial reporting, personnel and information management, as well as its ability to interface with larger systems. Therefore, we decided not to "reinvent the wheel", but to improve on the applicability of Apple microcomputer systems. Our plan involved creating a microcomputer network for administrative and fiscal reporting.

With the support of our Community School Board and District Superintendent, Marvin R. Aaron, we were ready to implement our microcomputer network design.

Networking refers to connecting several microcomputers together through a common transmission line and central source so as to allow the sharing of information and peripheral devices (mass storage, printer, modem).

Devices connected to a network have been termed "nodes" by network users. Currently, nodes must be intelligent. They must not be individual microcomputers or intelligent peripherals (printer/modem)1.

Current research defines three basic types of networks: Star, Daisy Chain, and Drop Line (Bus) 1,2. A microcomputer network constructed in Star configuration, consists of a central intelligent microcomputer, termed the host, with other devices connected in a radial or starlike pattern. All devices are directly connected to the host. If one device becomes inoperative, other devices still function. A Daisy Chain configurated network consists of a single host with all other devices wired in series to the host. If one device becomes inoperative, all devices past the inoperative device cease to funciton. The third network type, a Drop Line or Bus configuration, consists of a host with a single cable. All devices are connected in parallel to the main cable via junction boxes so that failure of any one device will leave the remainder of the system operative.

Our investigation of types of networks available for use with microcomputers led us to select the "Omninet" of Corvus Systems, Inc. 3 Omninet is constructed essentially in a Drop Line configuration, with each intelligent device connected to a hard disk storage system via an easily installed piece of hardware termed a "transporter". The advantage of this type of network is obvious, if a problem arises in one intelligent device, all other devices remain functioning. All intelligent devices share the resources of hard disk system. In addition, a primary intelligent device or host can control access of other users through a user defined security system, giving users (up to 64) different levels of access to information; read only, read and write and manager level access for security purposes. Therefore, our initial microcomputer network design consisted of the following equipment: 5 Apple II Plus (48k) Microcomputers with Language Cards, 5 Disk Drives with Controllers, 5 Zenith Data Monitors, 1 Qume 5 Printer, 1 Corvus 10 Megabyte Hard Disk System, 1 Corvus Disk Server, 8 Corvus Transporters, Panasonic Video Cassette Recorder (NV 8200) and D.C. Hayes Micromodem (see Appendix for approximate costs). Our financial commitment toward developing a microcomputer management network for district use was further supported through creating a district position of "Computer Specialist", that is, a person to provide support in implementing this network design.

To allow for rapid implementation of our management network, we chose to use commercially developed software packages developed for hard disk systems rather than have our Conputer Specialist develop customized management software (which would have delayed implementation over several months). These packages include DB Master (a data base management package), Word Handler (a word processing program) and Visicalc (a numerical data manipulation program). DB Master was selected for our data base management for several reasons, some of which include: automatic data compaction upon storage, sophisticated report generation and password protection system.

Let's take another step back and discuss methods of data base management. Data base management can be viewed as a pyramid structure. In a top/bottom structure, all information is collected by a central authority for creation of a data base. Subsequently, information is reported to collection sites for verification. In a bottom/top structured data base, each site manages its own data base. We used the floppy disk version of DB Master, which is, of course, compatible with the district hard disk version used for data base management. In a bottom/top configuration, each site shares its data base with the district producing a more accurate data base. Each site has a vested interest in management of its own information. Districts support each site and a cooperative working partnership has developed.

Each site manages its data base using the following equipment: Apple II Plus (48K) Micropcomputer with dual disk drives, Zenith Data Monitor, Epson MX 80 Printer and DB Master (floppy version). Recently, we have provided selected sites with Hayes Micromodems for eventual telephone hookups. Furthermore, for more efficient use of information management, sites are also adopting word processing using Word Handler (floppy version) which is interactive with our data base management program.

Our microcomputer management network functions to support the instructional process through various management applications, which include:

> word processing
> information storage and retrieval
> inventory
> mailing lists/labels

vendor reports
personnel records
student records
ad hoc reporting from larger data files

Individual microcomputers within the network can function independently, and with a small hardware attachment, can also function as a remote intelligent terminal with the Central Board of Education's IBM mainframe computer.

Recently, we have begun to experiment with an optical scanning device, the Scantron 2700, for mass entry of information into our data base. Eventually this device will minimize data entry time permitting immediate use of a data base at each participating site as well as facilitating creation of a master district data base.

Additional software applications for our network will be forthcoming; for example, we are investigating general accounting software (accounts payable, receivable, general ledger) which will be interactive with other programs. As an additional support to participating sites, we are investigating student attendance and scheduling programs that would be interactive with our student data base.

Lastly, one must consider confidentiality of information, security precautions and levels of access to information within a network. We have structured Omninet with four levels of security protection to authorize only approved users access to the network. First, Omninet only recognizes authorized users by an individual "name" assigned to each user; illegal users are denied access to the network by Omninet.

Once the network recognizes the user's "name", the user must then enter an identification code for further access to the network. Then, authorized users must place the DB Master Management Disk into the disk drive to access the data base management program stored within the hard disk system. Finally, the user must enter another password to gain access to data files. Once within the network, Omninet is structured to permit differentiated levels of access, that is, read, read and write, and manager level access to information.

If networking will best suit your management needs, then consider the following questions:

1. What is the greatest distance from one end of the network to the other?

2. What is the maximum number of microcomputers to be networked?

3. How much mass storage is required?

4. Which network offers capability for expanding or upgrading?

5. Are there current users that I can speak with?

6. What kind of service and support are available?

7. Is the manufacturer reliable?

8. Is the product supported by on-going development?

9. What is the cost of installation?

10. Can microcomputers of different manufacturers and/or peripherals be connected within the network?

References

1. Minnesota Educational Computing Consortium (MECC), "Spotlight on Local Networking with the Apple II Computer", September 1982.

2. Charp, Sylivia, "Trends-Time Sharing Microcomputers-Networking", *T.H.E. Journal*, November, 1981.

3. Corvus Systems,"Winchester Disk Systems for the Apple II", Corvus Systems, San Jose, California, 1982.

4. Connell, Cassie, "Networking, What are the Alternative Systems", *T.H.E. Journal*, September 1982.

Forman, Kenneth, and Steinhoff, Carl. "Networking for Microcomputer Management." From *Proceedings of National Educational Computing Conference,* 1983. Reprinted by permission.

Stage Six - Checklist

Organizing and Implementing for Success

When you have completed the following activities in Stage Six, you will have a completed, working plan for successful implementation of technology in your school system.

O   Develop and distribute a system policy on software duplication.

O   Provide for program coordination and implementation.

O   Provide for program evaluation.

O   Develop a logistical support system.

O   Develop materials and equipment support systems.

O   Plan for appropriate location and physical environment of equipment.

O   Provide for the security of equipment.

O   Develop and implement a process for scheduling, checkout and transfer of equipment.

From Preston, Stephen M. and Lee, Jane F. *Educational Planning Guide, Local Planning Guide.* Atlanta: Georgia State Department of Education. 1985.

Hardware Selection Tools

1. Hardware Evaluation Worksheet.

2. Stage Four -- Checklist

3.The Videodisk Production Worksheet

4. The Generic Disc: Realizing the Potential of Adaptive, Interactive Videodiscs.

Hardware Evaluation Worksheet

On the tally sheet below, assign an importance factor of 1 to 3 for each factor for each category, depending on how important you think each category is to your decision. The factor should be developed by your district committee and should be consistent as you rate various machines. **1 = Not important; 2 = Important; 3 = Very important.**

As you compared machines, give each one a rating of 1 to 3 in each category **(1 = Poor; 2 = Average; 3 = Good)**. For example, if dealer service is not available, give it a 1 under the "Service" category; if it is good, give it a 3. If no software is available, that category may be given a 1.

When all the categories have been rated, multiply them by the importance factor you originally assigned. The end results are then added together. The higher total will indicate the microcomputer best suited for your uses. Be as sincere as possible to get an unbiased evaluation. Color of the case, unnecessary extras, or the salesperson's personality should not affect the choice.

sample **Category**	**Importance** **Factor** **(1 to 3)**	**Rating** **(1 to 3)**	**Total**
Cost:			
Service:			
User Training:			
Brand:			

Category	Importance Factor (1 to 3)	Rating (1 to 3)	Total
Cost			
Service			
User Training			
System Expansion			
Flexibility			
Software			
Memory			
Keyboard			
Display			
Peripherals & Options			
Sound, Music, Voice, graphics			

Total_____

Reprinted by permission from *The Elements of Computer Education: A Computer Program,* 1983 Montana Office of Public Instruction.

Stage Four--Checklist
Selecting Software and Hardware

You should complete the following activities in Stage Four before you proceed to Stage Five in planning educational technology in your school system.

A software selection subcommitee has been appointed.

A system software review form has been developed.

The software review process has been developed.

Software has been located for review.

The software selection subcommittee is knowledgeable about systemwide goals for educational technology and existing software and its use in the system.

Software evaluation criteria have been developed and applied and software that meets system goals has been identified.

A hardware selection subcommittee has been appointed.

Funding options have been explored.

The hardware selection subcommittee have become familiar with state-of-the-art equipment.

Hardware selection criteria have been developed based on system goals and projected use.

Available equipment have been compared and rated and recommendations for purchase have been made.

The Videodisc Production Worksheet

Chad Worcester and Jim Smeloff

The videodisc Production Worksheet is a guideline by which an interactive videodisc project director can estimate the cost of a project.

To use the worksheet you must first determine how many hours of instruction/use you plan to provide the student/customer. Once that has been established you can approximate the number of stills (both videodisc and computer generated) needed by subtracting the amount of realtime video you plan to produce (one-sided disc, two-sided disc, etc.) from the hours of instruction/use you expect to provide. Be sure to account for any realtime video you know will be accessed more than once.Take the remaining time and divide by 15 seconds. This will give you the number of still frames you will need to produce.

In 1976, Junius Bennion determined that the average time for the use of a still frame in an interactive video program was 10 seconds. Because of the increasing complexity of interactive video content, we have revised that figure upward. However, the 15 seconds per still frame is not a hardset rule. You can change it according to your application.

Next, determine how many of these still frames will be generated solely from the videodisc, solely from the computer, or a combination of the two (computer overlay). With these calculations completed you will be able to determine how much realtime video you'll [sic] need to produce.

Plug these figures into the worksheet. Take notice of the footnote information. Before you find yourself spending wildly, the Videodisc Production Worksheet will give you a general idea of how much your proposed interactive videodisc project will cost to produce, exclusive of delivery system hardware.

It is a good idea to contract for a complete development package. A typical package includes interactive design (based on accepted instructional design models), the selection of a delivery system, the development of a script treatment and the preparation of a budget. These are the important elements of a proposed videodisc project and should be defined before any major production spending begins.

Remember, the Videodisc Production Worksheet is a guide. If you feel any of the dollar figures need to be adjusted according to your production circumstances feel free to do so. Also, these figures should be reviewed every six months and altered, if necessary, according to the fluctuations in the market.

Videodisc Production Worksheet

1. How many hours of instruction desired for interactive disc(s)__A__?

2. A minus realtime motion times 3600 = _____B_____.

3. B divided by 15(* 2) = C.

4. C = number of still frames (videodisc and computer).

5. C times 4(* 3) = D.

6. D = number of discframes needed for still frames.

7. D divided by 1800 = E.

8. E = realtime disc space needed for still frames.(* 4)

9. Initial contacts/consultation = (1%) of budget # 11 through 17. [of this list]

10. Development package (note 5) = 6% of budget #11 through 17.

	Level I	Level II	Level III
11. Final Design/Scripting (* 6).	$200/lm(*7)	$300/lm	$400/lm
12. Production/premastering(*8) video still frames(*9) realtime motion.	$16/still $2100/lm(*10) $1000/lm(*11)	$15/still $2100/lm $1000/lm	$13/still $2100/lm $1000/lm
13. Programming	-0-	$5/still	$15/still
14. Mastering (aver. price)(*13)	$2000	$2000	$2000
15. Replicating (aver price)(*14)	$18/disc	$18/disc	$18/disc
16. Project Evaluation(optional)	$150/lm	$150/lm	$200/lm
17. Packaging & Packaging Design	$5-20/unit	$5-20/unit	$5-20/unit

18. Contingencies = 10% of budget items #11 through 17.

19. Project Administration = 15% of budget items #11 through 18.

20. **Total Budget** _____

Notes

(1) Be sure to include any video segments that will be accessed more than once. Add that time to the real time motion amount. Also, take into account the disc space needed for still frames. See footnote #3.

(2) Each single frame will be viewed by the user for an average of 15 seconds.

(3) Each single frame will be laid down 4 times. This figure will vary according to the delivery system. This is a conservative figure for optical laser systems and a generous figure for capacitance systems.

(4) If you will be using more than 300 disc frames for still frames, you must plan carefully for the space they will take up on the disc.

(5) See the explanation about the development package in the accompanying comments.

(6) Includes time for instructional designer and writer.

(7) "lm" stands for linear minute of disc time. If your disc program is to be 25 minutes long (real time motion and still frames) then use this figure for multiplication.

(8) Includes cost for all production personnel.

(9) The production costs per still include design, photography, **character generation and digital video effects(DVE's).**

(10) This figure represents a high level of production, generally original production on 1" videotape with full 1" computer-controlled postproduction.

(11) This figure represents acceptable production elements, perhaps original production on 3/4" or professional 1/2" videotape.

(12) Multiply this figure by the total number of still frames (both videodisc and computer generated).

(13) These are average prices. You will need to contact the mastering house of your choice for the specific prices.

(14) See footnote #13.

From *The Videodisc Book* by Rod Daynes(Ed.) & Beverly Butler(Associate Ed.). New York: John Wiley and Sons, Inc., 1984, pp. 59. Reprinted by permission.

The Generic Disc: Realizing the Potential of Adaptive, Interactive Videodiscs

David H. Jonassen

There is little doubt that microcomputer-controlled interactive videodisc systems represent the most potentially powerful communication device in the history of instructional communications. Such systems are especially effective for engaging the learner in an interactive learning process and in adapting the mode, style, or instructional logic to accommodate individual differences in the learner with whom it is interacting.

The Socratic flexibility of the most creative teacher coupled with high-quality graphics, realistic video, and nearly instantaneous branching provides the possiblity of an infinite variety of adaptive sequences. Videodisc producers and designers have yet to conceive the sophistication of the tutorial and simulation instruction possible. The ability to adjust to any combination of learner characteristics in presenting instruction, to adapt to changing situations or characteristics, or to realistically simulate the outcome of various choices or behaviors sends goosebumps down the hides of instructional designers. The ability to provide truly equal educational opportunities to every learner would warm the heart of any humanist. Although I disdain bandwagons (as characteristic of the history of educational technology), this one just may be worth jumping on! If this is the case, however, why haven't we seen wider dissemination of this miracle medium?

The primary problem results from a fundamental conflict between education and economics - between the design potential of the interactive videodisc and the interests of educational publishers. First, the designers' side:

Instructional Potential

The interfacing of an optical videodisc player with a microcomputer represents the highest level of presentation possible for videodiscs. Beginning with linear play, sophistication increases through levels of user control, such as selecting sequences or frames, up to full micro computer control.

In essence, it marries the interactive flexibility of the computer, which enables designers to adapt instruction to meet an almost infinite variety of instructional needs, with the optical videodisc player, which can produce visual presentation in a greater variety than any existing visual display device.

This flexibility makes it especially useful for adaptive, interactive instruction. By adaptive, I mean able to adapt or adjust the presentation sequence,mode, or sign type to meet a variety of instructional requirements, such as the learner's instructional needs, prior knowledge, content/task type. Instructional designs could be based on curricular needs or matching models of instruction derived from aptitude-treatment interaction research. It is possible to address several of these levels of adaptation within the same program.What this would entail is presenting an alternative version or sequence of instruction. For instance, alternative versions of different programs could be accessed, depending upon whether a person was an inductive or a deductive reasoner and what objective he or she wished to acquire. By interactive, I mean that the program engages the learner to participate in the instructional process in a variety of ways that utilize learner responses and feedback algorithms, i.e., to establish a computer-learner dialogue based upon the types of learner differences you wish to accommodate.

The potential exists for producing computer-disc courseware that tailors instruction to the needs of the individual--the holy grail of individualized instruction programs for the past two decades.

Two Problems Exist. First, adaptive principles of instruction based upon aptitude-treatment interaction (or task-treatment interaction) research do not generalize. The interactions among and between aptitude variables and instructional conditions are so complex as to render generalizations impossible (Snow, 1977). At best, we can hope to develop local theories of instructional situations concerned with limited portions of the curriculum. Even that is beyond the capability of all but a few of the best-supported school districts or industries with close ties to university research facilities (Gehlbach, 1979).

Second, development costs for interactive video-discs are phenomenally high. Including the labor costs for instructional designers programmers, producers, and talent, production costs for mastering an interactive videodisc appear to begin at $100,000 for the most basic computer-disc program with only limited interaction and adaptation. Elaborate programs which fully utilize the potential of the medium would cost several times that figure. A series may be done more cheaply, but the cost will remain very high. If these adaptive, interactive programs do not have universal applicability, the development costs will be prohibitive, because they will have to be spread over so few copies, since sales would be so limited. Not even the best-endowed industrial or military facility can afford to begin to cover their curriculum or even a small part of it with interactive disc instruction designed consistent with their local theories of instruction when the development costs are so high. The medium most adaptable to the needs of any specific instructional situation turns out to be beyond the means of virtually all of them!

Publisher Demands

Many publishers have expressed very restrained interest in interactive videodisc instruction. Their enthusiasm is dampened by at least two limitations of the interactive videodisc phenomenon.

First, the pilot projects producing interactive videodisc instruction have produced a lot of isolated prototypes in order to display the potential of the medium, but the publishers want to see series of programs (Sustik, 1983).

Second, we are all aware of the economic exigencies of the publishing business that result in the claims of cradle-to confirmation applicability of instructional materials, since publishers need to spread the front-end development costs plus profit. This is the obvious reason for the high purchase price of films, because of the low number of anticipated sales.

The entertainment industry, on the other hand, is mass-producing both capacitive and optical discs for sale in the $20-$40 range. They need only to buy the rights, press a master (so to speak, since optical mastering is a complex process), and produce thousands of copies at a price that thousands of individuals can afford. The joint ABC/NEA School disc project can afford to do the same for linear play instructional discs. But if your courseware is adaptive and interactive, which limits its applicability to local situations and increases the development costs exponentially, then sales will be limited and the per unit cost astronomical. These limitations are further exacerbated by the variety of microcomputer formats (at least 30) and video-discs formats (as many as 14, though not all of those are adaptable to computer control or have been produced in sufficient numbers) for which courseware would have to be adapted.

It simply is not feasible to market adaptive, interactive, computer-controlled videodisc courseware that even begins to tap the potential of the medium or cover the curriculum of schools, businesses, or the military. Pilot projects will continue to produce exciting and effective prototypes, but the widespread dissemination of the technology is likely to be compromised by its own potential and the economic constraints of the educational marketplace.

Solution: The Generic Disc

A potential solution to this conflict between economics and educational potential is "the generic disc." The solution is simple — let local designers/teachers program their own adaptive, interactive discs to meet their own local instructional needs and idiosyncracies using generic content discs produced and distributed by publishers.

Publishing Generic Discs

Generic discs would consist of up to 29 and 1/2 minutes of instructional video programming per side. The additional half minute, or 900 frame displays, like a menu (table of contents), chapter or unit headings, narrative overviews or summaries, blank screens for superimposing titles from the computer, and so on. Rather than producing an edited sequence designed to be viewed in a linear manner, such as broadcast video, generic discs could be broken down and presented in a variety of standard sequences that reflect the structure of subject matter.

If we assume that subject matter structures provide an important basis for sequencing content (Reigeluth, Merrill, and Bunderson, 1978), then discs or series of discs can be organized using appropriate structures (e.g., linear for factual or descriptive content, hierarchial for concept content, etc.), using a consistent content organization or disc structure for each disc or series, each disc might contain an introduction, a variety of content sequences organized globally by type of content structure, a review, and, of course, a menu (content list), chapter introductions, and so on.

Rather than designing content chapters using subject matter structures, publishers simply may want to present different versions of the same content using alternative global learning strategies. For instance, the same content could be presented in an inductive sequence, as suggested before, and then in a deductive sequence. An option might show processes using alternate presentational strategies. For instance, a disc teaching a procedure may show each step of a process once from an objective camera angle and once from a subjective camera angle, or repetition of the procedure using a long shot, medium shot, and close-up. The point is that the publisher would not be required to engage in developing and programming expensive adaptive, interactive designs — that would be left to the local purchaser. Rather, the publisher could produce series of discs using a few, consistent formulae for arranging content of the discs. In fact, by segmenting sequences using these heuristics, producers would not even be required to edit their programs as extensively as they need to do in order to provide the continuity necessary for linear play. Production costs for the publishers would be minimal. They could use stock film and video, do some basic organization and arrangement, produce graphics using a character generator and aster and sell the discs at a cost affordable to most schools and businesses. What publishers are avoiding are the expensive, labor-intensive costs of instructional development necessary to arrange and program interactive videodiscs.

With minimal effort, video produced for broadcast or linear play could be adapted as a generic disc. In fact, local programming of linear play discs is possible, though considerably more difficult and not nearly as flexible. If an optical linear play disc can be produced for sale in the $20-$30 range, a generic disc should be possible for $30-$35.

The User

If the local designer/educator could have access to a collection of quality generic discs covering a significant portion of his or her curriculum, the hardware and software costs necessary for locally programming interactive videodiscs would be easily justifiable. It is affordable. Assuming that the local school, business, or education agency already owns a micrcomputer (Apple, Atari, Commodore, IBM-PC,

North Star, TRS-80, or others) and a laser reflective disc player (Pioneer and Sony consumer or industrial models are the· most common), then you need only two additional components to make even a rank neophyte capable of the most sophisticated programming.

First, you need a microcomputer videodisc player interface, available from a variety of manufacturers (see the following article, by Prof. Dean Zollman). This is the unit that translates output from the computer into input commands which control the disc player. They sell from $295 up to a few thousand dollars with a median price of less than $500.

Next, you need an authoring system, which is microcomputer software that uses a very high level language to convert user commands into machine language commands for controlling the disc player after prompting the user to provide the necessary information. Systems, such as PILOT Plus (available from On Line Computer Systems) or IN-SIGHT Plus (from Whitney Educational Services) will work with most microcomputers and disc players (see Table 1). These enable the educator/designer with no computer programming experience to quickly learn how to achieve the most sophisticated interactive options. It would be helpful for such a person to have some instructional design training or experience in order to fully utilize the potential of such a system, but the procedure is simple. After booting the authoring system, the designer is prompted to type in adjunct introductory material, such as organizers, overviews, or periodic inserted material, such as inserted questions and directions to use strategies (e.g., take notes, map materials, generate images).

Directions are entered to access and play various segments or individual frames of the disc. The disc segments, identified by frame numbers one to 54,000 can be played at regular speed, still frame, slow motion, or rapid search. You might want to pause in the middle of a video sequence to point out the position of a particular object, repeat part of a sequence, and then resume play at normal speed.

As a designer, the authoring system and micrcomputer interface will provide you with full control of the contents of the videodisc for an additional investment of around $1,000 or less. Excited? Read more.

A local designer could adapt his or her disc, using a microcomputer and authoring system software, to produce some of these suggested options to learners:

Learner Control—Giving learners options about which sequences they want to view or the order in which they want to see them.

Remediation—By inserting questions and using remedial algorithms, learners could be branched back through sequences having been given additional directions, information, analogies, organizers, strategies, etc., using the microcomputer.

Grade level/Curricular Adaptation—The same disc could be adapted and readapted to meet different grade-level requirements or to provide support for programs with different curriculum emphasis.

Prior Knowledge—Pretest the learners with the microcomputer program and adapt the sequence according to the student's prior knowledge.

Adapt to Learner Styles—Programs could be developed to adapt the instruction to accommodate different learner styles. For instance, a compensatory design for impulsive learners might require them to respond to more thoughtful questions or to employ generative strategies which require them to relate new materials to existing knowledge. A capitalization design for field independents might provide them with opportunity to outline or map a course of instruction, while field dependents should be compensated by the provision graphic organizers or structured overviews of the program.

Program Control—Adapting instruction based on algorithms programmed by the designer.

Many other options are possible. The same videodisc could be adapted in any number of ways. The only additional cost for each program would be $3.00 or so for another floppy disc to store the additional program.

Summary

The concept of the generic disc would make the most flexible and powerful adaptive instructional medium available to a wider audience. It would put responsibility for adapting the basic instructional program encoded on the videodisc to local instructional needs right where it belongs – at the local level. Based upon the needs or styles of learners in a particular location, adaptive, interactive video instruction could be inexpensively developed that would maximize the learning potential of all types of learners. If local learning problems require local solutions, the use of microcomputer-videodisc interfaces and authoring systems would enable local designers to solve their local instructional problems in creative, productive ways. Since generic discs could provide sophisicated video programming at prices affordable to most education agencies, adequate incentives to publishers to produce a variety of generic discs could be provided by the market-place. The production of generic videodiscs for local programming would symbiotically team publishers and schools/businesses in a way that would potentially benefit not only both of them but also the learners of this nation.

Table 1

Videodisc Authoring Systems

1. On Line Computer Systems
20251 Century Blvd.
Germantown, Maryland 20874
(301) 428-3700
PILOT Plus contains built-in support for control of all optical videodisc players. Available or planned for the TRS-80, Apple II with Z80 card, North Star, Altos, Cromemco, Datapoint 1550, Intel Multibus, Hewlett Packard 14=50, Xerox 820, IBM-PC and look alikes, Unix and Unix look-alikes, DEC PDP11/xx, and Rainbow 350.

2.Whitney Educational Services
1499 Bayshore Highway
Burlingame, CA 94010
(415) 570-7917

INSIGHT Plus system for the Apple IIe and Sony SM70 ($895) and IBM-PC ($995)

3. Apple Computer Company
20525 Mariani Avenue
Cupertino, CA 95014
(408) 996-1010
Super PLIOT will drive most popular VCR and optical videodisc players; lists for $200 (management system extra).

4. WICAT Systems, Inc.
P.O. box 539
1875 South State
Orem, Utah 84507
(801) 224-6400
WISE System includes graphics editor and animation; Menu-driven; runs on WICAT 68000 micro.

References

Gehlbach, R.D. Individual Differences: Implications for Instructional Theory, Research, and Innovation. *Educational Researcher*, 1979 8(4), 8-14.

Reigeluth, C.M., Merrill, M.D., and Bunderson, V.V. The Structure of Subject Matter Content and Its Instructional Design Implications. *Instructional Science,* 1978, 7, 107-127.

Snow, R.E. Individual Differences and Instructional Theory. *Educational Researcher,*1977,6,11-15.

Sustik, J. Personal Communication, March 6, 1983.

from: Jonassen, David "The Generic Disk: Realizing the Potential of Adaptive, Interactive Videodiscs." *Educational Technology,* 23No.1 (January 1984):21-14. Reprinted by permission.

Software Selection and Evaluation Tools

1. General Information.

2. Short Form Software Evaluation.

3. Instructional and Technical Design of Software.

4. Software Evaluation Resources.

5. A Checklist for Evaluating the Instructional Design of Educational Software.

6. Lesson Evaluation Tool.

7. Software Evaluation Criteria

8. Evaluating Software.

9. How to Review Software.

10. Levels of Evaluation for Computer-Based Software.

11. Computer-Managed Instruction Evaluation.

General Information

1. Product Name: _____

2. Source: _____

3. Cost: _____

4. Written for:

___ Apple
___ Commodore
___ TRS-80
___ Atari
___ Sinclair
___ Osborne
___ IBM
___ Data General
___ Digital
___ Texas Instruments
___ (Other) _____

5. Program Intent:

___ Computer-Managed Instruction
___ Computer-Assisted Instruction
___ Word Processing
___ Class Scheduling
___ Attendance Recordkeeping
___ Administrative Budgeting/Recordkeeping
___ Administrative Reporting-School
___ Administrative Reporting-District
___ (Other)_____

6.User:

   ___ Teacher
   ___ Teacher Aide
   ___ School Administrator
   ___ District Administrator
   ___ Clerical Aide
   ___ Content Specialist
   ___ Pupil Personnel Specialist
   ___ Student
   ___ Grade Levels

7. System Required:

   ___ 16K
   ___ 32K
   ___ 48K
   ___ 64K
   ___ 1 Disk Drive
   ___ 2 Disk Drive
   ___ Tape
   ___ Printer
   ___ Graphics Tablet
   ___ Color Monitor
   ___ Card Reader
   ___ (Other)_____

8. Subject Area: _____

9. To Accompany: _____

10. Defined Purpose: _____

11. Type of Data Entry:

   ___ Keyboard
   ___ Card Reader
   ___ Graphics Tablet
   ___ (Other)_____

12. Functions:

___ Test Scoring
___ Data Analysis
___ Prescriptions
___ Recordkeeping
___ (Other)_____

13. Reports:

___ Class Roster
___ Attendance Records
___ Report Card Grades
___ Assignments for Individual Students
___ Individual Educational Plans
___ Report of Test Results by Student/Group
___ Report of Activity Completion by Student/Group
___ Supplemental Activity Completion by Student/Group
___ Level Mastery Results by Student/Group
___ Teacher-Made Test Results by Student/Group
___ Correlation with Local Objectives
___ Complete Record of Individual Student Performance on Activities
    and Tests
___ Parent Report
___ Group Report by Item Performance
___ Group Performance by Objective
___ Longitudinal Report of Group Performance
___ (Other)_____

14. Accompanying Support Materials

___ Manual
___ Tests

15. Handling of User Problems

___ Hotline
___ Replacement Disks

16. Procedure for Backing-Up Disks:

___ Not Possible
___ Copy Disk
___ (Other)_____

User Orientation

(Following each item, provide space for: Poor, Fair, Good, or Excellent check marks, plus room for comments)

17. Clarity of Directions

18. Consistency of Directions

19. Style/Language of Directions

20. Readability of Screen Displays

21. Attractiveness of Screen Displays

22. Readability of Reports

23. Completeness of Report Content

24. Usefulness of Information Provided by Reports

25. Freedom from Need for External Directions/Information

26. Usefulness of Program (Screen) Reaction to Inappropriate Entries

27. Efficiency of Procedure to Correct User Errors

28. Flexibility of System

29. Efficiency of Procedures for User Control of Rate/Sequence of Presentation

30. Efficiency of Procedures to Revise Entries

31. Effectiveness of Support Materials

32. Comprehensiveness of Support Materials

33. Provision for Special (Shortcut) Features

34. Operative/Response/Calculating Time of Program

35. Freedom from Bias (Sex, Culture, etc.)

36. Overall Ease of Use

Summary Evaluation

37. Does the software achieve its defined purpose?

38. What use do you see for the program in its target setting (e.g., classroom)?

39. What are the program's noteworthy strengths?

40. What are the program's noteworthy weaknesses?

41. Would you use or recommend the use of this software?
___ Yes
___ Yes, with reservation
___ No
Please comment on the reason for your answer:

From "Computer Managed Instruction Evaluation" by William Phillip Garth and Paula M. Nassef, *Educational Technology Magazine*, January, 1984, pp. 31-32. Reprinted by permission of publisher.

Short Form Software Evaluation

Program Name: _____

Subject Area: _____

Grade Levels: _____   Ablilty Levels: _____

1. What specific content or instructional objectives are addressed?
(Use back of form if necessary)

2. Has the program been tested or validated for a classroom setting?
Yes   No

3. Is the program correlated with test materials? Yes   No

4. Are test materials required for program use? Yes   No

5. Description and cost of text materials

6. Is program available for review before purchase? Yes   No

7. Computer requirements:
Brand & Model _____
Memory Requirement _____K
Operating System _____
Individual Computer ( )   Network ( )

Peripherals required:
    ( ) Printer   ( ) Joy Stick   Disk drives (How many?)____
    ( ) Color Monitor   ( ) Graphics Tablet
    ( ) Other _____

8. Media on which program is available:

  ( ) Disks (size & type) _____

  ( ) Cassette/Cartridge tape (type)_____

  ( ) Other _____

9. Producer: _____

10. Price $_____   Vendor _____

J.E. Eisele

Computer-Assisted Instruction Readiness Checklist

Instructions: The following 25 items represent both instructional design and technical design criteria for a well-developed CAI lesson. As you review your lesson, check for the pressence or absence of these attributes. A negative response signals need for a possible modification of the lesson.

yes no

( ) ( ) 1. Specific skills, knowledge, or abilities required for a learner to interact with the lesson have been specified.

( ) ( ) 2. The learner knows what is expected of him or her, that is, objectives have been clearly identified.

( ) ( ) 3. A test is included at the beginning of the lesson for diagnostic purposes.

( ) ( ) 4. The lesson is structured so that a learner may interact with all or part of the lesson as appropriate for his or her abilities.

( ) ( ) 5. The lesson presents new information in a context that directly relates what the learner already knows to the new material.

( ) ( ) 6. The lesson is organized so that the learner acquires basic skills before attempting to demonstrate more advanced skills.

( ) ( ) 7. A variety of explanations has been presented.

( ) ( ) 8. Exercises, problems, or questions are provided for the learner to practice the types of skills, attitudes, or knowledge specified by the objectives.

( ) ( ) 9. The lesson is written in such a way as to provide clues to key concepts (use of asterisks, underlining, etc.).

( ) ( ) 10. Outlines, summaries, or reviews are provided to help the student organize key ideas.

( ) ( ) 11. A variety of different questioning formats (multiple choice, matching, true-false, completion) are utilized.

( ) ( ) 12. Questions elicit responses relevant to the content being presented.

yes no

( ) ( ) 13. Restatement of important concepts is provided to learners to reinforce learning.

( ) ( ) 14. When a learner answers incorrectly, feedback is provided to suggest what information appropriate responses should induce.

( ) ( ) 15. Vocabulary appropriate for the learner has been used.

( ) ( ) 16. A posttest is included to determine learner achievement of stated objectives.

( ) ( ) 17. The learner knows what to do; any specific procedures for interacting with the computer terminal have been explained.

( ) ( ) 18. Opportunities for frequent interaction between learner and computer have been provided.

( ) ( ) 19. The learner is informed about his or her status (score, how many lessons completed, etc.).

( ) ( ) 20. The typing skills necessary to make a response have been minimized.

( ) ( ) 21. Flexibility in accepting learner responses, especially synonyms, has been developed.

( ) ( ) 22. Opportunities for assistance within the lesson (as HELP, RESTART, and REVIEW) are available.

( ) ( ) 23. The lesson is not so lengthy as to be tiring.

( ) ( ) 24. Any supplementary materials necessary for the use of the lesson are provided for the learners.

( ) ( ) 25. The lesson is different than a textbook lecture, or programmed instruction book.

Module _____ Name _____

PLATO File Name_____   Date _____

Software Evaluation Resources

The Best of Apple Software, Ltd.
The Best of Atari Software, Ltd.
The Best of Commodore Software, Ltd.
The Best of Texas Instruments, Ltd.
Publications International, Ltd.
3841 W. Oakton Street
Skokie, IL 60076
(312) 67604370

Each of these guides include an education section with 140 to 200 entries. Programs are evaluated by user groups and are rated on a scale of one to ten.

Conduit
P.O. Box 388
Iowa City, IA 52244
(319) 355-5789

Courseware Report card
Educational Insight
150 W. Carob Street
Compton, CA 90220
(213) 979-1955

Separate issues have been published for the Apple, Atari, Commodore, IBM and TRS-80 computers, as well as separate editions for elementary and secondary levels. Every issue contains evaluations and summaries.

Course reviews 1984
SMERC Library Microcomputer Center
San Mateo County Office of Education
333 Main Street
Redwood City, CA 94603
(415) 363-5472

Fifty programs in all curriculum areas are evaluated in this publication of the San Mateo Educational Resource Center (SMERC). These reviews, compiled by educators, describe each program and note strengths, weaknesses, student responses and a checklist of evaluator criteria.

The Digest of Software Reviews: Education
School and Home Courseware, Inc.
Suite C
1341 Bulldog Lane
Fresno, CA 93710
(209) 227-4341

The Digest profiles instructional software programs, including administrative programs for Apple, Atari, IBM, and TRS-80. Each issue reviews 50 programs which have been heavily reviewed in journals and newsletters.

Disc Compendium
Carol Klenow
Disk Project Manager
11CD, Oakland Schools
2100 Pontiac Lake Road
Pontiac, MI 48054
(313) 858-1895

The DISC Compendium, produced by the interactive and instructional computing Department of the Oakland County Schools, is a collection of 91 software evaluations and documentations for PET, Apple, and TRS-80 computers.

Educational Micro Review
P.O. Box 14445
Austin,TX 78761
(512) 345-0001

Each month Educational Micro Review summarizes articles from more than 25 Microcomputer publications and includes over 300 reviews. Areas covered include hardware, software, networks, robotics, books, films, tapes, and information utilities.

Evaluation of Educational Software: A Guide to Guides
Publications Office
Southwest Educational Development Laboratory
211 East Seventh Street
Austin, TX 78701

This is a useful reference guide for teachers and administrators who are responsible for software evaluation.It provides information on 10 evaluation systems, including abstracts and sample forms from MicroSIFT, EPIE/Consumers Union, MECC, and the National Council of Teachers of Mathematics.

Evaluator's Guide for Microcomputer-Based Instructional Packages
International Council for Computers in Education
University of Oregon
1787 Agate Street
Eugene, OR 97403

This guide was developed by MicroSIFT to be used with the MicroSIFT rating scale.

Guidelines for Evaluating Computerized Instructional Materials
National Council of Teachers of Mathematics
1906 Association Drive
Reston, VA 22091

This publication includes guidelines to use in reviewing software, a sample form to use in requesting software information from publishers and a sample form to use in evaluating documentation.

The Journal of Courseware Review
Foundation for the Advancement of Computer-Aided Education
20863 Stevens Creek Blvd.
Building B-2, Suite A-1
Cupertino, CA 95014

Media Review 172 Holmes Road P.O. Box 425
Ridgefield, CT 06877
(203) 438-2843

Each issue of this monthly publication includes microcomputer software evaluations covering a specific subject area. Program reviews are cumulatively indexed by title, publisher, and, subject.

Micro CO-OP
P.O. Box 432
West Chicago, IL 60815
(312) 232-1984

Micro Courseware/Hardware Pro/Files and Evaluations
EPIE Institute
P.O. Box 839
Water Mill, NY 11976
(516) 283-4922

Pro/Files are 2 to 4 page software evaluations covering all major curriculum areas and grade levels. These reviews include analyst's summary, capsule evaluation, user comments, sample frames, student's comments, and other instructional value and documentation evaluation.(These materials are available to each Georgia school system through Instructional Media Services, Georgia Department of Education.)

Microcomputer Software and Information for Teachers (MicroSIFT)
Northwest Regional Educational Laboratory (NWERL)
500 Lindsay Building
300 SW 6th Avenue
Portland, OR 97204
(503) 248-6800

Micrcomputers in Education
Queue, Inc.
5 Chapel Hill Drive
Fairfield, CT 06432

RICE (Resources in Computer Education)
BRS, Inc.
1200 Rt. 7
Latham, NY 12110
(518) 783-7251
(800) 833-4707

RICE is an on-line information database, part of the Northwest Regional Educational Laboratory's MicroSIFT project.

The database includes information on approximately 2,000 software programs for use in elementary and secondary schools. The RICE database is available to subscribers to Bibliographic Retrieval Services.

School Microware Review
Dresden Associates
P.O. Box 246
Dresden, ME 04342

The Software Exchange
Technical Education Research Centers
8 Eliot Street
Cambridge, MA 02130
(617) 547-3890
Contact: Tim Barclay

Software Reports
Allenback Industries, Inc.
2102 Las Palmas
Carlsbad, CA 92008
(619) 438-8694
(800) 854-1515

The nearly 400 software programs listed in this directory have been evaluated by an independent team of teachers and administrators. Each entry includes a description of the program and vendor information. The directory is updated twice each year.

Softswap
c/o Ann Lathrop
San Mateo County Office of Education
333 Main Street
Redwood City, CA 94063
(415) 363-5472

This is one of the best known educational software clearinghouses.

Whole Earth Software Review
150 Gate Five Road
Sausalito, CA 94965
(415) 332-4335

This quarterly guide presents the comparative surveys of software and
hardware products that the Whole Earth research staff has tested and
recommends. A compilation of the reviews can be purchased in the
Whole Earth Software book published by Doubleday

From Preston,Stephan M. and Lee, Jane F. *Educational Planning
Guide, Local Planning Guide*. Atlanta: Georgia State Department of
Education, 1985.

A Checklist for Evaluating the Instructional Design of Educational Software

Objective: What should the software teach your students to do:

The Question: How well and how efficiently do students who have used the program learn the skills specified above?*

1. Does the software require a high frequency of responding [as opposed to screens of material to read]? For tutorials and drills, how many problems does a student actually do in a 10-minute period?

2. Is the responding relevant to your goals? [Do students do what they are to learn?]

3. Do students have to respond to the critical parts of the problem?

4. Is most of the screen content necessary for the response, or does the program assume that students will learn content without having to respond overtly to it?

5. Does each screen ask students to discriminate between at least two possible responses?

6. Can students see their progress as they work with the program [as opposed to becoming frustrated]? Do they enjoy using the program?

8. For series of lessons to be used repeatedly: Does the program adjust according to the performance level or progress of the student?

* The best way to judge an instructional program is, of course, to try it out with students. Even without trying a program out, however, you can usually spot programs with weak instructional design so that you can eliminate them from those your students try.

From: Vargas, Julie S. "A Checklist for Evaluating the Instructional Design of Educational Software." *The Kappan*, Vol. 67, No. 10, June 1986, p. 744. Reprinted by permission.

Lesson Evaluation Tool

Part I. Overall lesson including both computer and non-computer components.

DIRECTIONS:

1. Circle a number on the scale next to each instructional event indicating how closely you believe the success of your lesson correlates with the statement provided.

2. As you consider each event, note any suggestions that may occur to you for modifying the lesson.

Lesson Title: _____

Lesson Objective(s): _____

Instructional Events	Event Rating Scale	Modifications Needed
	low high	
Gaining Attention	1 2 3 4 5	This activity helped students to focus on task.
Informing student of Objectives	1 2 3 4 5	This activity helped students form expectations about the need to master content to be presented.
Stimulate recall of Prerequisite knowledge	1 2 3 4 5	This activity helped refresh students' memories of related information.
Presenting content	1 2 3 4 5	The content presentation was clear and accurate.
Providing Learning Guidance	1 2 3 4 5	This activity provided effective instructional support for the student.
Eliciting Performance	1 2 3 4 5	The practice or application activities reinforced new knowledge.

Part II. Computer-related activities.

DIRECTIONS:

1. Using the scale below as a reference, circle a number indicating your response to each of the following statements.

2. Where appropriate, add suggestions for improvement and comments.

Activity Title _____

Scale	**Statement**
low high	**Instructional**
1 2 3 4 5	The computer component helped students to achieve the lesson objectives.
1 2 3 4 5	The software used accommodated the range of student abilities.
1 2 3 4 5	Students were interested in the computer activity.
1 2 3 4 5	The software proved to be a valuable component of the lesson.
	Classroom Management
1 2 3 4 5	The grouping arrangement used was successful.
1 2 3 4 5	The time required for the computer-related portion of the lesson was appropriate.
1 2 3 4 5	The technique used for student monitoring was effective.
1 2 3 4 5	Students were able to operate the hardware.
	Software
1 2 3 4 5	A sufficient quantity of the software was available to meet lesson needs.
1 2 3 4 5	The software ran without any problems.
1 2 3 4 5	The software made effective use of the computer as an instructional medium.
	Hardware
1 2 3 4 5	A sufficient quantity of hardware was available.
1 2 3 4 5	All the appropriate hardware was available.

From Lesson Evaluation Tool by Grefory, Carrier and Glenn in *The Computer Teacher,* vol. 13, no. 8, May 1986. Permission not required-a CopyMe publication.

Software Evaluation Criteria and Rating Scale

Criteria	Rating

Instructional Design Features

1. Target population identified.	1 2 3 4 5
2. Learning needs addressed.	1 2 3 4 5
3. Objectives clearly stated.	1 2 3 4 5
4. Pre requisites specified.	1 2 3 4 5
5. Stimulus displayed.	1 2 3 4 5
6. Frequent responses required.	1 2 3 4 5
7. Prompts provided.	1 2 3 4 5
8. Response judging.	1 2 3 4 5
9. Content logic.	1 2 3 4 5
10. Content scope/sequence.	1 2 3 4 5
11. Practice provided.	1 2 3 4 5

System Features

12. Ease of use.	1 2 3 4 5
13. Documentation	1 2 3 4 5
14. Special Features.	1 2 3 4 5
15. Friendliness.	1 2 3 4 5
16. Writing level, style.	1 2 3 4 5
17. Humor.	1 2 3 4 5
18. Needed peripherals identified.	1 2 3 4 5
19. Cost.	1 2 3 4 5
20. Ability to modify.	1 2 3 4 5

Scale: 1 = low quality, 5 = high quality.

By: James E. Eisele, 1984

Evaluating Software

A. Student use	Yes	No
1. Requires no computer knowledge	___	___
2. Does not require student reference to manuals	___	___
3. Loading instructions clear; loading program easy to load	___	___
4. Available menu: can user select?	___	___
5. Instructions given so as to skip if user needs	___	___
6. Effective feedback for correct response	___	___
7. Effective feedback for incorrect response	___	___
8. Positive reinforcement more attractive than negative reinforcement	___	___
9. Keys chosen to perform operations located wisely on keyboard	___	___
10. User's control over the rate of presentation	___	___
11. Accepts abbreviation for common responses (i.e., Y for yes)	___	___
12. Provides user with summary of performance	___	___

B. Instructor use	Yes	No
1. Instructional objectives clearly stated	___	___
2. Easily integrated into curriculum	___	___
3. Ability to change rate and difficulty of material	___	___
4. No need for teacher assistance	___	___
5. Useful teacher manual and/or accompanying materials provided	___	___
6. Suggested lesson plans	___	___
7. Suggested grouping arrangements	___	___
8. Follow-up activities suggested	___	___
9. Provides whole class summaries of performance	___	___
10. Clear, nicely formatted screens	___	___
11. Bug-free: program runs properly	___	___

[Author unknown]

How To Review Software

Basic Questions for all Software

1. Subject area

2. Microcomputer

3. Topics

4. Grade level (estimate)

5. Program name

6. Author

7. Publishers

8. Copyright date

9. Publisher address

10. Disk/cassette/cartridge

11. Type of package: single program - part of a series - other

12. Price

13. Additional hardware required

14. Additional software required

15. Grouping arrangements: individual__ small group__

16. Type of program: drill practice__ tutorial__ simulation__
educational game__ arcade game__

17. Other _____

[Author unkown]

Levels of Evaluation for Computer-Based Software

Strand 1

1. The introductory lesson made it easy to use the computer.
YES   NO   NOT SURE

2. The computer is difficult to use.
YES   NO   NOT SURE

3. I think I can learn a lot with this.
YES   NO   NOT SURE

4. I would rather learn this material in a regular class than with this computer.
YES   NO   NOT SURE

5. Have you ever learned from a computer before?
YES   NO   NOT SURE

6. I would like to take more lessons on the computer.
YES   NO   NOT SURE

7. The computer was available when I wanted to use it.
YES   MOST OF THE TIME   SOME OF THE TIME

8. The lessons have encouraged me to improve my basic skills.
YES   NO   NOT SURE

9. The computer allows me to work at my own pace.
YES   MOST OF THE TIME   SOME OF THE TIME

10. I tried to just finish the lesson rather than learn the material.
YES   MOST OF THE TIME   SOME OF THE TIME

STRAND 2

1. I like using the computer.
USUALLY- SOMETIMES-NEVER

2. I am learning a lot with this computer.
YES   NO   NOT SURE

3. I would rather learn this material in a regular class than with this computer.
YES   NO   NOT SURE

4. The lessons challenge me to do my best work.
YES   MOST OF THE TIME   SOME OF THE TIME

5. Taking the tests helped me know if I really understood the material.
YES   MOST OF THE TIME   SOME OF THE TIME

11. The computer always seems to be breaking down.
YES   MOST OF THE TIME   SOME OF THE TIME

12. Someone was available to help me when there were computer failures or other problems
USUALLY-SOMETIMES-NEVER   NOT SURE

13. For [me], most of the work in these lessons was.
VERY DIFFICULT   DIFFICULT   ABOUT RIGHT

14. [Should the Army] continue to develop lessons for the computer?
YES   NO   NOT SURE

15. I can use what I learned from these lessons on the job.
YES   NO   NOT SURE

From *Instructional Software* by Walker and Hess ©1984 by Wadsworth, Inc. Used by Permission.

Computer-Managed Instruction Evaluation Form

Date:..

Reviewer:.......................................

General Information

1. Printer name: ....

2. Source:.......................................

3. Cost:...

4. Written for:
.... Apple
.... Commodore
.... TRS-80
.... Atari
.... Sinclair[1]
.... Osborne[1]
.... IBM
.... Data General
.... Texas Instruments
.... (Other)................................

5. Program intent:
.... Computer-managed instruction
.... Computer-assisted instruction
.... Word Processing
.... Class scheduling
.... Attendance recordkeeping
.... Admin budgeting/record keeping
.... Admin reporting-school
.... Admin reporting-district
.... (Other)................................

6. User:
.... Teacher
.... Teacher aide
.... School administrator
.... District administrator
.... Clerical aide
.... Content specialist
.... Pupil personnel specialist
.... Student

7. System Required:
..... 16K .....32K 64K
..... 1 disk drive....2 drives
..... tape .....printer
..... graphics tablet
.... color monitor
..... card reader
..... (other)................................

8. Subject area:..............................

9. To accompany:.........................

10. Defined purpose:....................

11. Type of data entry:
.... Keyboard
.... Card Reader
.... Graphics tablet
.... (other)................................

12. Functions:
.... Test scoring
.... Data analysis
.... Prescriptions
.... Record keeping
.... (other)................................

13. Reports:
.... Class roster
.... Attendance records
.... Report card grades
.... Assignments for individuals
.... Individual educational plans
.... Report of test results by
          students/group
.... Report of activity completed
          by student/group
.... Supplemental activity com-
          pletion by student / group
.... Level mastery results by
          student / group
.... Teacher-made test results
          by student / group
.... Correlation with local
          objectives
.... Complete record of
          individual student
          performance on
          activities and tests
.... Parent report
.... Group report by item
          performance
.... Group performance by
          objectives
.... Longitudinal reports of
          group performance
.... (other)...............................

14. Accompanying support
materials:
.....Manuals
.....Tests

15. Handling of user problems:
.....Hotline
.....Replacement disks

16. Procedure for backing-up
disks:
.....Not possible
.....Copy disk
.....(other).............................

User Orientation

(Following each item, provide space for: Poor, Fair, Good, or Excellent check marks, plus room for comments.)

17. Clarity of directions
18. Consistency of directions.
19. Style / language of directions.
20. Readability of screen display
21. Attractiveness of screen display
22. Readability of reports
23. Completeness of report contents.
24. Usefulness of information provided by reports
25. Freedom for need for external direction/information
26. Usefulness of program (screen)
27. Efficiency of procedures to correct user errors

28. Flexibility of system
29. Efficiency of procedures for user control of rate/materials
30. Efficiency of procedures to revise entries
31. Effectiveness of support
32. Comprehensiveness of support materials
33. Provision for special (short-cut) features
34. Operative/response/calculating time of program
35. Freedom from bias(sex, culture, etc.)
36. Overall ease of use

Summary Evaluation

37. Does the software achieve its defined purpose?

38. What use do you see for the program in its target setting (e.g., classroom)?

39. What are the program's noteworthy strengths?

40. What are the program's noteworthy weaknesses?

41. Would you use or recommend the use of this software?
.... Yes
.... Yes, with reservations
.... No
    Please comment on the reason for your answer:

Reprinted by permission from *Educational Technology Magazine,* Vol. XXIV, No. 1, pp. 28-32.

Staff Development

1. Planning for Staff Development.

2. Technology Staff Development.

Stage Five - Checklist

Planning for Staff Development

You should complete the following activities in Stage Five before you proceed to Stage Six [Organizing and Implementing] in planning for educational technology in your school system.

O   Identify competencies necessary to implement technology sucessful-ly in your schools.

    O   Administrative

    O   Teachers

    O   Clerical

    O   Support personnel

O   Determine who needs training for which competencies.

O   Plan for and project costs associated with ongoing staff development.

O   Develop specific specific staff deveelopment activities and accompanying timelines for first year.

O   Develop general objectives and timelines for staff development for second and third years.

O   Plan for and begin to implement appropriate evaluation, follow-up and support activities.

From Preston, Stephen M. and Lee, Jane F. *Educational Planning Guide, Local Planning Guide*. Atlanta: Georgia State Department of Education. 1985.

Technology Staff Development Outline

Following is *one* suggested outline for a staff development program for your school district. Feel free to use it as is or to modify it to suit your school district's needs.

I. Technology Awareness
    A. Terminology

    B. Concepts

II. Brief History of Technology (See Chapter II)
    A. First Revolution

    B. Second Revolution

    C. Third Revolution

    D. Fourth Revolution

III. Hardware Components and How They Work
    A. Computers

    B. Videodisk

    C. Telecommunications

IV. Software
    A. Operating System Software

    B. Applications Software

    C. Programming Software

V. Administrative Applications
    A. Word Processing

    B. Data Base Applications

    C. Electronic Spreadsheet

    D. Shared Databases

VI. Instructional Support/Management Applications
    A. Classroom Records Management

    B. Testing/Scoring

    C. Diagnosis/Prescription

VII. Direct Instructional Applications
    A. Computer Assisted Instruction

    B. Computer Based Instruction

VIII. Evaluating Software
    A. Characteristics of Good Software

    B. Evaluation Criteria

    C. Evaluation Forms

IX. Programming *Overview* (In-Depth instruction seperate)
    A. BASIC

    B. LOGO

    C. PASCAL

If you don't intend to train all staff at once, you may wish to modify this agenda to fit each audience.

Eisele, UGA.

Technology Curriculum Resources

1. Curriculum and Instructional Resource List.

2. Elementary Keyboarding.

Curriculum and Instructional Resource List

Anderson, Ronald E., and Klassen, Daniel L. "A. Conceptual Framework for Developing Computer Literacy Instruction." *AEDS Journal,* Volume 4, Number 3, Spring, 1981.

Computer Literacy Curriculum Guide: Grades K-9 St. Paul: Minnesota School Districts Data Processing Joint Board (TIES), September 1982, pp. 12-50.

Cupertino Union School District. "K-9 Computer Literacy Curriculum," *The Computing Teacher*, March 1983, pp. 7-10.

Grady, M. Tim. "Long-Range Planning for Computer Use." *Educational Leadership*, May 1983.

Hunter, Beverly., Dearborn, Donald, and Snyder, Bruce. "Computer Literacy in the K-8 Curriculum." *Phi Delta Kappan*, October 1983.

Hunter, Beverly. *My Students Use Computers: Learning Activities for Computer Literacy.* Reston, VA: Reston Publishing Company, Inc., 1983. See particularly Chapters 3 through 7.

From Preston, Stephan M. and Lee, Jane F. *Educational Technology: Local Planning Guide.* Atlanta: Georgia State Department of Education, 1985.

Elementary Keyboarding-Is It Important?*

by

Truman H. Jackson and Diane Berg

As computers become a common element in the elementary school, a major question posed is, "How do I make elementary students more efficient in the use of the keyboard ?" The answer is, "Provide an appropriate instructional sequence in keyboarding."

In an early, informal analysis of student key efficiency using the "hunt and peck" method versus keying efficiency after 15 hours of appropriate keyboarding insruction, students with instruction were judged to be approximately twice as fast as those who had no formal keyboarding instruction. This judgment was made by a computer science instructor who had some students in a programming class directly following their keyboarding instruction and some students who had not yet received keyboarding instruction.

If a school has a computer education program with sufficient hardware, the decision to teach keyboarding has potential to either reduce the number of computers required in a school or allow students more productive time at the computer after only 15 hours of appropriate keyboarding instruction. From either perspective, increased efficiency or reduced cost, a formal keyboarding sequence makes sense. Therefore, a formal elementary keyboarding instructional program must be given consideration equal to other key computer decisions, such as hardware purchase and software selection.

What is appropriate keyboarding instruction? Answers to the following questions will help in the creation of a keyboarding instructional sequence which will provide each student an opportunity to develop reasonable keyboarding skills.

Are keyboarding and typewriting the same? Keyboarding, simply defined, is learning the correct manipulation of the keys on a computer/typewriter keyboard and using that keyboard for basic data input. Typewriting is the continued development of keying skills and the use of those skills to produce output in a variety of applications, such as in the creation of letters, memoranda and reports.

Should keyboarding be taught? The incorporation of computers into the classroom and the introduction of application software in early elementary grades make reasonable keyboarding skills necessary. Using a computer without properly learning keyboarding skills will definitely hinder their future development.

Where should keyboarding be taught in the curriculum? Keyboarding should be taught just prior to required use of the keyboard for text entry, the inputting of words and/or numbers such as in keying word lists, creating sentences, entering programs, or using a word processor.

In early elementary (K-12), the goal of instruction may simply be to aid students in locating keys on the keyboard. But beginning at about the third grade level, formal development of correct keyboading technique should be introduced, focusing on the alphabetic keys. Third grade students are physiologically ready to learn keyboarding and studies have shown that they can become keyboard proficient. At the upper elementary level, number and symbol/funtion keys should be introduced along with a simple-to-use text editor/word processor.

Where does the time come from for keyboarding insruction? In most cases, time for keyboarding insruction is coming from language arts. Since keyboarding has great potential to contribute to language arts skills development–learning new words and word definitions and creating spelling lists, sentences and paragraphs--it is frequently the subject area into which keyboard instruction is integrated. Social studies is another common area through which keyboarding instruction is offered.

How much time is needed for keyboarding instruction? Feedback from ongoing programs indicates that approximately 30 hours of instruction at the elementary level-15 hours in each of two consecutive grades or 10 hours each in three consecutive grades-provides the most successful teaching/learning sequence. Twenty-to 30-minute class periods which meet every day work best for elementary students. Weekly 30-minute review sessions should continue throughout the year to help assure continued use of proper technique and keying skills.

What materials should be used? Both computer software and textbooks are available for keyboarding insruction. Since either set of materials can be used, hardware availability and instructor expertise tend to influence choice of materials.

Computer Aided Instructional (CAI) software for keyboarding has become more sophisticated. Some of the more recent software programs include instruction for correct technique; paced skill development where all input is monitored by keystroke, by word, or by line; speed reports beginning in early lessons; continuous, positive, relevant feedback; motivational devices such as games and printable progress reports; and an option for open screen keying where material keyed in may be printed. A combination of CAI software and a keyboarding textbook, which have coordinated lessons, provide the most desirable instructional media. Where both software and text are used, lines in each should be coordinated lesson-by-lesson so a student may switch from a computer to a typewriter at any time and can continue a lesson or drill using the same drill material.

Several examples of software packages which incorporate some or all of these criteria are: Microtype, The Wonderful World of PAWS, MECC Keyboarding Primer, Alphabetic Keyboarding and Superkey. MicroType, The Wonderful World of Paws, with the coordinated text. Computer Keyboarding, An Elementary Course meets all of the above criteria. In MicroType, the Wonderful World of PAWS, special emphasis is placed on the use of integrated screen graphics to teach correct keyboarding technique, the area of instruction which is most critical for beginning learners. The program is based on sound pedagogical keyboarding insruction, while being fun and motivational for the user.

MECC Keyboarding Primer and Alphabetic Keyboarding also use integrated graphics to teach correct keyboarding technique. Superkey has a separate lesson devoted to technique insruction. The level of technique instruction varies among programs based on the age of student the program was designed to serve. Alphabetic Keyboarding is designed for grades 7 through 12, so the technique instruction is more inclusive and goes beyond basic body, finger and eye position. Each of these programs teaches correct manipulation of the alphabetic keyboard and also provides drill and practice for the development of basic keying skills. As instructor you must evaluate keyboarding software carefully to determine how you will use it to help meet the instructional needs of your students.

What equipment should be used? Either computers or electric/electronic typewriters, or a combination of both, may be used, but computers are generally preferred at the elementary level. Manual typewriters are inappropriate.

Does furniture size make a difference? Furniture is an important, often overlooked, consideration. Both table height and chair height must match student size to ensure that students can reach the keyboard properly. In cases where furniture does not match student size and cannot be modified or adjusted, cushions and footrests may be needed so proper body position is possible.

Who should teach keyboarding? Elementary teachers and high school typewriting teachers are teaching keyboarding at the elementary level. The keyboarding instructor should have a high interest in teaching keyboarding and have taken a methods course in keyboarding/typewriting. The methods course for business teachers should aid them in working with elementary-age students. Elementary teachers must learn keyboarding skills. At the junior and senior high levels, a qualified business education typewriting teacher is the appropriate instructor.

What should be taught? Initial instruction should include correct keyboarding technique and the alphabetic keyboard. To maximize use of limited time, early learning should concentrate on correct manipulation of the alphabetic keyboard. Equally important is correct keyboarding technique, which includes body position, keystroking, and operation of the space, return and shift keys.

What procedures should be used? The first two or three sessions should include orientation and then presentation of the home-row keys. Two new keys should be introduced each day thereafter. During the teaching/learning process, students must be monitored constantly and given immediate, appropriate feedback regarding what they are doing right and wrong. Students must be encouraged to make corrective adjustments immediately, particularly in technique, so bad habits are not formed. Understanding and using correct techniques are the most critical learning elements in beginning keyboarding.

Early drills must be short, usually in the eight- to 15-second range. Speed rather than accuracy, should be emphasized. Error correction should be allowed, using the back arrow. The development of keystroking sequences (chaining) should be encouraged as soon as key reaches are learned. A variety of activities and constant involvement of the instruction, in drills and in evaluation/feedback, are key ingredients which will contribute to the success of keyboarding instruction for both student and instructor. Activities should include, but not be limited to: teacher-called keystrokes (as in teaching of a new key), teacher-dictated words, student-called words (make up from the keys already learned), student composition based on presented phrases (e.g., Complete the following sentence), creation of poems, new-key learning exercises, skills reinforcement lines, appropriate skill reinforcement games, etc.

How should keyboarding performance be evaluated? Evaluation must focus on correct technique, the critical teaching/learning component of beginning keyboarding, through observation of students as the key . If a student is doing well, or if incorrect technique is being used, the teacher should tell him/her immediately. A technique check sheet, similar to that provided in the *Teacher's Guide for MicroType,* The Wonderful World of PAWS, page 12, would be helpful as an evaluation aid and in keeping track of student progress. When speed is checked, students should be encouraged to improve-try to type a little faster this week than last week. Self competition of this type is recommended, but competition between students see who can type the fastest is not appropriate; generally, three or more errors should be allowed per line of type.

Should instruction be graded? A pass/fail grading system should be used. Letter grades should not be given since all evaluation (correct technique and keying skill) is done on a subjective basis. Rewards such as certificates, stars, stickers, etc., for various accomplishments should be given out daily and/or weekly to students. A reward system will help generate enthusiasm, build interest, and increase motivation. After the keyboarding unit, a certificate of completion should be given to each student.

Development of a keyboarding sequence based on consideration of each of these concerns will help assure the success of the program, and the success of your keyboarding program will add to the success of your entire computer curriculum.

(For more specific information about the implementation of keyboarding contact the authors. Truman H. Jackson, Business Education Programs Specialist, Minnesota State Department of Education, St. Paul, MN 55101; Diane Berg, Instructor, Crestwood Elementary School, East Grand Forks, MN 56723.)

Software

Alphabetic Keyboarding, Jackson, Schroeder, Haugo, South-Western Publishing Co., Cincinnati, OH 1983.

The Electronic Keyboard for Personal and Business Use, Minnesota Curriculum Services Center, St. Paul, MN, 1984.

MECC's Keyboarding Primer, Minnesota Educational Computing Corporation, St. Paul, MN 1985.

MicroType, The Wonderful World of PAWS, Haugo, Hausmann, Jackson, South-Western Publishing Co., Cincinnati, Oh, 1985.

Superkey, LaVinge, Rutledge, Howell, Bytes of Learning Incorporated, Toronto, Ontario, Canada, 1985.

References

The Electronic Keyboard for Personal and Business Use, Minnesota Curriculum Services Center, St. Paul, MN, 1984.

Computer Keyboarding An Elementary Course, Crawford, Erickson, Beaumont, Robinson, Ownby, South-Western Publishing Co., Cincinnati, OH, 1985.

*From *The Computing Teacher,* March 1986, pp. 8-11. Reprinted by permission.

Sources of Software

Sources of Software

Abbott Educational Software
334 Westwood Avenue
East Longmeadow, MA 01028

Academic Software
22 E. Quackenbuch Av.
Dumont, NJ 07628
(201) 385-2395
Apple, TRS-80, PET, Vic, Atari

Activity Resources Company,
Inc.
P.O. Box 4875
Hayward, CA 94540
(415) 782- 1300
TRS-80, Apple, PET

Addison-Wesley Publishing Co.
Reading, MA 01867
(617) 944-3700
Apple, IBM, TRS-80-III

Ahead Designs
699 N. Vulcan,#88
Encinitas, CA 92024
(619) 436-4071
Apple

American Micro Media
P.O. Box 306
Red Hook, NY 1257
(914) 756-2557
Apple, Pet, TRS-80

Apple Computer, Inc.
10260 Bandley Drive
Cupertino, CA 95014
(408) 996-1010
Apple

Applied Educational Systems
RFD 2, Box 213
Dunbarton, NH 03301
(603) 774-6151
Apple, Pet. TRS-80

Applied MicroSystems
P.O. Box 832
Roswell, GA 30077
(404) 371-0832
Apple, IBM

Aquarius Publishers, Inc.
P.O. Box 128
Indian Rocks Beach, FL 33535
(813) 595-7890
Apple, TRS-80

Arthroid Digital, Inc.
P.O. Box 1385
Tittsfield, MA 01202
(413) 448-8278
Apple

Avant-Garde Creations
P.O. Box 30160
Eugene, OR 97403
(503) 345- 3043
Apple, IBM, Atari

Banana, Inc.
P.O. Box 2868, 3400 Executive
Pky.
Toledo, OH 43606
(419) 531- 7100
Apple, Atari, IBM

Bank Street College of Education
610 West 112th St.
New York, NY 10025
(212) 663-7200
Apple, Atari, Commodore 64

Basics and Beyond, Inc.
P.O. Box 10, Pinesbridge Road
Amawalk, NY 10501
(914) 962- 2355
Atari, TRS-80 I & II

Bell & Howell Microcomputer
7100 N. McCormick Road
Chicago, IL 60645
(312) 673-3300
Apple

Borg-Warner Educational Systems
600 W. University Dr.
Arlington Heights, IL 60004
(800) 323-7577
Apple, TRS-80

BrainBank, Inc.
Suite 408, 220 Fifth Avenue
New York, NY 10001
(212) 686-6565
Apple, TRS-80, PET

Broderbund Software
1938 4th Street
San Rafael, CA 94901
(415) 456-6424
Apple, Atari

COMP.O.S.E.
6500 W. 95th St.
Oak Lawn, IL 60453
(312) 599-5550
Apple

COMPress
P.O. Box 102
Wentworth, NH 03282
(603) 764-5831
Apple

California School for the Deaf
39350 Gallaudet Dr.
Fremont, CA 94538
(415) 794-3666
Apple

Charles Mann and Associates
7594 San Remo Trail
Yucca Valley, CA 92284
(619) 365-9718
Apple, IBM

Compu-Tations, Inc.
P.O. Box 502
Troy, MI 48099
(313) 689-5058
Apple II, Atari 800

Computer Advanced Ideas, Inc.
1442A Walnut Street, Suite 3 1
Berkeley, CA 94709
(415) 526-9100
Apple, IBM

Computer Software/Books R US
16 Birdsong
Irvine, CA 92714
(714) 559-5120
Apple, Atari, Pet, TRS-80, IBM

Computer Station
11610 Page Service Dr.
St. Louis, MO 63141
(314) 432-7019
Apple

Computers to Help People, Inc.
1221 West Johnson Street
Madison, WI 53715
(608) 257-5917
Apple II Plus

Concept Educational Software
P.O. Box 6184
Allentown, PA 18001
(215) 266-1679
TRS-80 Mod I or II

Conduit
100 Lindquist Center
University of Iowa
P.O. Box 388
Iowa City, IA 52244
(319) 353-5789
Apple, TRS-80, Atari, PET

Control Data Publishing Co.
P.O. Box 261127
San Diego, CA 92126
(800) 233-3784
Apple, Atari, Texas Instruments

Convergent Systems Inc.
245 E. 6th St.
St. Paul, MN 55101
(612) 221-0587
TI, Apple

Cow Bay Computing
P.O. Box 515
Manhasset, NY 11020
(516) 365-4423
PET, Comm-64

Cross Educational Software
P.O. Box 1536
Ruston, LA 71279
(318) 255-8921
Apple

Data Command
P.O. Box 548
Kankakee, IL 60901
(815) 933-7735
Apple, TRS-80 I & III

Developmental Learning
Materials
One DLM Park
Allen,TX 75002
(214) 248-6300
Apple IIe, TI-99/4A

Dormac, Inc.
8034 S.W. Nimbus
Beaverton, OR 97005
(800) 547-8032
Apple

Duxbury Systems, Inc.
77 Great Road
Acton, MA 07120
(617) 263-7761
CP/M

Dynacomp, Inc.
1427 Monroe Avenue
Rochester, NY 14618
(716) 442-8960
Apple, Atari, IBM,
TRS I & III, PET 64

Joseph Nichols Publisher
P.O. Box 2394
Tulsa, OK 74101
(918) 583-3390
TRS-80 Model III

Carl Geigner
1603 Court Street
Syracuse, NY 13208
Apple II

EDIS Systems, Inc.
422 Main Street
Lafayette, IN 47901
(317) 742- 1787
Apple II, TRS-80, Mod III

EISI
2225 Grant Road
Los Altos, CA 94022
(415) 969-5212
Apple, Atari, TRS-80, TI, PET

EX-ED Computer Systems, Inc.
71-11 112th St.
Forest Hills, NY 11375
(212) 269-0020
any running CP/M

Early Games Educational
Software
Shelard Plaza North, Suite 140C
Minneapolis, MN 55426
(612) 544-4720
Apple II, Atari, IBM, TRS-80

Earthware Computer Services
Box 30039
Eugene, OR 97403
(503) 344-3383
Apple

Edu-Comp, Inc.
14109 S.E. 168th St.
Renton, WA 98005
(206) 255-7410
Apple

Edu-Soft
4639 Spruce Street
Philadelphia, PA 19139
(215) 747-1284
Apple II, Atari, TRS-80

Edu-Ware Services
28035 Dorothy Drive
Agoura, CA 91301
(213) 706-0061
Apple, Atari, IBM

EduTech
634 Commonwealth Ave.
Newton Centre, MA 02159
(617) 965-4813
Apple

Educational Activities, Inc.
P.O. Box 392
Freeport, NY 11520
(800) 645-3739
Apple, PET, TRS-80, Atari

Educational Computing Systems, Inc.
136 Fairbanks Road
Oakridge, TN 37830
(615) 483-4915
Apple II

Educational Micro Systems, Inc.
P.O. Box 471
Chester, NJ 07930
(201) 879-5982
TRS-80 I & III, Apple

Educational Software and
Marketing
1035 Outerpark Drive
Springfield, IL 62704
(217) 787-4594
Apple, TRS-80 III

Educational Software, Inc.
4565 Cherryvale
Soquel, CA 92630
(408) 476- 4901
Atari, Comm-64, Vic

Educational Systems Software
P.O. Box E
El Toro, CA 92630
(714) 768-2916
Apple

Educational Teaching Aids
159 W. Kinzie
Chicago, IL 60610
(312) 644-9438
Apple, Commodore, TRS-80

Educulture
1 Dubuque Plaza, Suite 803
Dubuque, IA 52001
(800) 553-4858
Apple

Edupro
P.O. Box 51346
Palo Alto, CA 94303
(415) 494-2790
Atari

Eiconics, Inc.
P.O. Box 1207, 211 Cruz Alta Rd.
Taos, NM 87571
(505)758-1696
Apple

Electronic Courseware Systems
P.O. Box 2374, Station A
Champaign, IL 60820
(217) 359-7099
Apple

Elwyn Institutes
111 Elwyn Road
Elwyn,PA 19063
(215) 358- 6400
TRS-80 Mod. III

Encyclopedia Britannica Ed.
Corp.
425 N. Michigan Ave.
Chicago, IL 60611
(800) 554-9862

Entelek
P.O. Box 1303
Portsmouth, NH 03801
(603) 436-0439
Apple

Evans Newton Inc.
7745 E. Redfield Road, Suite 100
Scottsdale, AZ 85160
(602) 998-2777
Apple, PET, TRS-80

Financial Analysis Service
P.O. Box 1937
Hiram, OH 44234
(216) 569-3201
Apple

Fireside Computing, Inc.
5843 Montgomery Road
Elkridge, MD 21227
(301) 796-4165
TRS-80 or III

Follett Library Book Co.
4506 Northeast Highway
Crystal Lake, IL 60014
(800) 435-6170

Fullmer Association
1132 Via Jose
San Jose, CA 95120
(408) 997-1154
Apple

Funk Vocab-Ware
4825 Province Line Road
Princeton, NJ 08540
(609) 921-0245
Apple II

GRAFex Company
P.O. Box 1558
Cupertino, CA 95015
(408) 996-2689
Atari

George Earl Software
1320 South Gen. McMullan
San Antonio, TX 78237
(512) 434-3681
Apple, TRS-80

Gladstone Electronics
901 Fuhrmann Blvd.
Buffalo, NY 14203
(716) 849-0735
Timex Sinclair

Green Valley Informantics
769 N. Sacre Lane
Monmouth, OR 97361
(503) 838-1172
PET, CBM

Grover and Associates
7 Mt. Lassen Dr. D116
San Rafael, CA 94903
(415) 479-5906
Apple II or II Plus

Harcourt Brace Jovanovich
1250 6th Avenue
San Diego, CA 92101
(800) 543-1918
Apple, TRS-80, Atari

Harper & Row
10 East 53rd Street
New York, NY 10022
(212) 593-7000
Apple

Hartley Courseware, Inc.
P.O. Box 431
Dimondale, MI 48821
(616) 942-8987
Apple

Instructional/Comm Tech Inc.
10 Stepar Place
Huntington Station, NY 11746
(516) 549-3000
Apple

Hayden Book Company, Inc.
600 Sussolk
Lowell, MS 01853
(800) 343-1218
Apple, Atari, PET

J&S Software, Inc.
140 Reid Avenue
Port Washington, NY 11746
(516) 944-9304
Apple, TRS-80 I & III

Holt, Rinehart, and Winston
383 Madison Avenue
New York, NY 10017
(212) 872-2000
Apple, PET, TRS-80

J.L. Hammett
Box 545
Braintree, MA 02184
(800) 225-5467
Apple, Atari, IBM, PET, TRS-80

IOR Enterprises
Rt.6, Box 20
Chapel Hill, NC 27514
(919) 92904825
Apple II Plus

JMH Software
4850 Wellington Lane
Minneapolis, MN 55442
(612) 559-4790
Atari, Commodore PET, VIC, 64

Ideatech Company
P.O. Box 62451
Sunnyvale, CA 94088
(408) 985-7591
Apple

Jagdstaffel Software
608 Blossom Hill Road
San Jose, CA 95123
(408) 578-1643
Apple

Information Unlimited Software
281 Arlington Avenue
Berkeley, CA 94707
(415) 331-6700
Apple, IBM, TI

Jamestown Publishers
P.O. Box 6743
Providence, RI 02490
(401) 351-1915
Apple II & IIe

Instant Software
Peterborough, NH 03458
(800) 343-0728
Apple, TRS-80, TI, PET

K-12 Micromedia
P.O. Box 17
Valley Cottage, NY 10989
(201) 391-7555
Apple, Atari, TRS-80, I, III, PET

Krell Software Corporation
1320 Stony Brook, NY 11790
(516) 751-5139
Apple, Atari, TRS-80 I & III,
Com. PET & 64

Bruce Land & David Farmer
395 Brooktondale Road
Brooktondale, NY 14817
Apple II

Lara Software
980 Hunting Valley Place
Decatur, GA 30033
(404) 634- 7601
Apple

Laureate Learning Systems, Inc.
1 Mill Street
Burlington, VT 05401
(802) 862-7355
Apple II

Learning Company
4370 Alpine road
Portola Valley, CA 94025
(415) 851-3160
Apple, Atari, TRS color

Learning Systems
P.O. Box 15
Marblehead, MA 01945
(617) 639-0114
Apple II, DEC, IBM, TRS-80

Learning Systems, Ltd.
P.O. Box 9046
Fort Collins, CO 80525
(303) 482-6193

Learning Tools
686 Massachusetts Ave.
Cambridge, MA 02139
(617) 864-8086
Apple II & III, IBM, DEC

Learning Tree Software, Inc.
Box 246
Kings Park, NY 11754
(516) 462-6216
Pet, Commodore 64

Learning Well
200 South Service Road
Roslyn Heights, NY 11577
(516) 621-1540
Apple II

Lightning Software
P.O. Box 5223
Stanford, CA 94305
(415) 327-3280
Apple, Atari, IBM-PC

Love Publishing
1777 South Bellaire St.
Denver, CO 80222
(303) 757-2579
Apple II

MARAC
280 Linden Avenue
Branford, CT 06405
(203) 481-3271
Apple, Atari, TRS-80, Comm.

MCE, Inc.
157 S. Kalamazoo Mall
Kalamazoo, MI 49007
(616) 345-8681
Apple II, IIe

Mean (Ed. Turnkey Systems)
256 North Washington St.
Falls Church, VA 22046
(703) 536-2310
Apple, IBM, TI

MECC (Minn. Ed. Comp. Consortium)
2520 Broadway Drive
St. Paul, MN 55113
(612) 638-0627
Apple, Atari

MIND
50 Washington Street
Norwalk, CT 06854
(203) 846-3435
Apple II, TRS-80

MUSE (Micro Users Software Exchange)
347 Charles Street
Baltimore, MD 21201
(301) 659-7212
Apple, Atari

Mathware
919 14th Street
Hermosa Beach, CA 90254
(213) 379-1570
Apple II

McGraw-Hill Gregg Division
1221 Avenue of the Americas
New York, NY 10020
(800) 223-4180
Apple, TRS-80

McKiligan Supply Corp. Dist.
435 Main Street
Johnson City, NY 13790
(607) 729-6511
Apple, TI, Atari, IBM, Comm.

Media Materials, Inc.
2936 Remington Avenue
Baltimore, MD 21211
(301) 235-1700
Apple, TRS-80 III

Merit Micro Software Corp.
404 Texas Commerce Bank Bldg.
Asmarillo, TX 79101
(806) 353-7888

Merlan Scientific Ltd.
247 Armstrong Avenue
Georgetown, Ontario
Canada L7G 4X6
(416) 877-0171
Apple, PET

Merry Bee Communications
815 Crest Drive
Omaha, NE 68046
(402) 592-3479
Apple

Metrologic Publications
143 Harding Avenue
Bellmawr, NJ 08031
(609) 933- 0100
Apple, TRS-80, PET

Micro Computer Service, Inc.
2885 East Aurora Ave., Suite 14B
Boulder, CO 80303
(303) 447-9471
CP/M

Micro Lab Learning Center
2310 Skokie Valley Road
Highland Park, IL 60035
(312) 433-7550
Apple, IBM

Micro Learningware
P.O. Box 307
Mankato, MN 56001
(507) 625-2205
Apple, TRS-80 III, PET

Micro Power & Light Company
12820 Hillcrest Road, Suite 224
Dallas, TX 75230
(214) 239-6620
Apple

Micro-Ed, Inc.
P.O. Box 24156
Minneapolis, MN 55424
(612) 926-2292
Apple, TI, Comm

MicroGnome (Div. of Fireside)
5843 Montgomery Rd.
Elkridge, MD 21227
(301) 796-4165
TRS-80, CPM

Microcomputer Workshops
103 Puritan Drive
Port Chester, NY 10573
(914) 937-5440
Apple, Atari, TRS-80, PET,
Comm 64

Microcomputers Corporation
P.O Box 8
Armonk, NY 10504
(914) 273-6480
Texas Instruments

Micrograms, Inc.
P.O Box 2146
Loves Park, IL 61130
(815) 965-2464
PET, Vic

Micromatics, Inc.
181 No. 200 West, Suite 5
Bountiful, UT 84010
(801) 292- 2458
Apple, TRS-80

Microphys Programs
2048 Ford Street
Brooklyn, NY 11229
(212) 646-0140
Apple, TRS-80, PET, Comm 64

Microsoft Services
P.O. Box 776
Harrisonburg, VA 22801
(703) 433-9485
TRS-80 III

Midwest Software
Box 214
Farmington, MI 48024
(313) 477-0897
Apple, PET

Milliken Publishing Company
1100 Research Blvd.
St. Louis, MO 63132
(314) 991-4220
Apple, Atari

Milton Bradley
443 Shaker Road
East Long Meadow, MA 01028
(413) 525-6411
Apple, TI

Mount Castor Industries
368 Shays Street
Amherst, MA 01002
(413) 253-3634
Apple, TRS-80, Comm.

Msss D., Inc.
3412 Binkley
Dallas, TX 75205
(214) 522-8051
Apple

Musitronic
P.O. Box 441, 555 Park Drive
Owatonna, MN 55060
(507) 451-7871
Apple

N.I.R.E., Don Selwyn
97 Decker Road
Butler, NJ 07405
(201) 838-2500
TRS-80 I & III

Nova Software
P.O. Box 545
Alexandria, MN 56308
(612) 762-8016
Apple II

Opportunities For Learning, Inc.
8950 Lurline Avenue Dept. 26C
Chatsworth, CA 91311
(231) 341-2535
Apple, TRS-80, Atari, PET

Orange Cherry Media
7 Delano Drive
Bedford Hills, NY 10507
(914) 666-8434
Apple, Atari, PET, TRS-80

PIE, Inc.
1714 Illinois St.
Lawrence, KS 66044
(913) 841-3095
Apple

Personal Software, Inc.
(Visicorp)
2895 Zanker Road
San Jose, CA 95134
(408) 946-9000
Apple, IBM

Potomac MicroResources, Inc.
P.O. Box 277
Riverdale, MD 20737
(301) 864-4444
Apple II

Powell Associates, Inc.
3724 Jefferson, Suite 205
Austin, TX 78731
(800) 531-5239
Apple, CP/M, TRS-80 I & III

Powersoft
P.O. Box 157
Pitman, NJ 08071
(609) 589-5500
Apple

PracEd Tapes, Inc.
12162 SE 14th St.
Bellevue, WA 98005
(206) 747-8485
Commodore

Precision People, Inc.
P.O. Box 17402
Jacksonville, FL 32216
(904) 642-1980
TRS-80 I & III

Problem Solving Through
Strategy
Olivia Public School
Olivia, MN 56377
(612) 523-1031
Apple

Program Design, Inc.
11 Idar Court
Greenwich, CT 06830
(203) 661-8799

Programs For Learning, Inc.
P.O. Box 954
New Milford, CT 06776
(203) 355-3452
Apple, TRS-80, PET

G. Evan Rushakoff
New Mexico State University
Las Cruces, NM 88003
(505) 646-2801
Apple II

Prentke Romich Company
8769 Township Road 513
Shreve, OH 44676
(216) 567-2906
Apple II

Quality Educational Designs
P.O. Box 12486
Portland, OR 97212
(503) 287-8137
Apple, TRS-80, PET, Comm 64

Queue, Inc.
5 Chapel Hill Drive
Fairfield, CT 06432
(800) 232-2224
Apple, Atari, Comm., TRS-80

Radio Shack (Education
Division)
1600 Tandy Center
Fort Worth, TX 76102
(817) 390-3302
TRS-80 all models

Raised Dot Computing
310 S 7th Street
Lewisburg, PA 17837
(717) 523-6739
Apple

Random House School Division
400 Hahn Road
Westminster, MD 21157
(800) 638-6460
Apple, TRS-80

Readers Digest
Pleasantville, NY 10570
(914) 769-7000
Apple, Atari, TRS-80

Quality Educational Software
P.O. Box 502
Troy, MI 58099
(313) 689-5059
Apple. Atari

Reston Publishing Company
11480 Sunset Hills Road
Reston,VA 22090
(800) 336-0338
Apple, Atari

Rocky Mountain Software, Inc.
214-131 Water Street
Vancouver, B.C.
Canada V6B 4M3
Apple II

SEI (Sliwa Enterprises, Inc.)
P.O. Box 7266,2013
Cunningham Drive
Hampton, VA 23666
(804) 826-3777
Apple

SLED Software
P.O. Box 16322
Minneapolis, MN 55416
(612) 926-5820
PET

San Juan Unified School District
6141 Sutter Avenue
Carmichael, CA 95608
(916) 944-3614
Apple

Scholastic Software
904 Sylan Avenue
Englewood Cliffs, NJ 07632
(212) 944-7700
Apple, Atari, PET, TRS-80, TI

School & Home Courseware,
Inc.
1341 Bulldog Lane, Suite C
Fresno, CA 93710
(209) 227-4341
Apple II

Science Research Associates,
Inc.
155 North Wacker Drive
Chicago, IL 60606
(800) 621-0664
Apple, Atari, TI

Scott, Foresman Elec. Publishing
1900 East Lake Avenue
Glenview, IL 60025
(312) 399-8877
Apple

Serendipity Systems, Inc.
419 W. Seneca St.
Ithaca, NY 14850
(607) 277-4889
Apple

Sierra On Line
36575 Mudge Ranch Road
Coarsegold, CA 92714
(800) 845-8688
Apple, Pet, TRS-80

Sof/Sys, Inc.
4306 Upyon Ave. So.
Minneapolis, MN 55410
(612) 929-7104
Apple II, IBM

Softswap
333 Main Street
Redwood City, CA 94063
(415) 363-5470
Apple, public domain programs

Software Connections, Inc.
1800 Wyatt Drive, Suite #17
Santa Clara, CA 95054
(408) 988-3704
Apple

Software Research
P.O. Box 1700
Victoria, BC
Canada VFW 2Y2
(604) 477-7246
Apple, IBM

Software Technology, Inc.
3763 Airport Road
Mobile, AL 36608
(205) 344-7600
Apple, IBM, CP/M

SouthWest EdPsych Services
P.O. Box 1870
Phoenix, AZ 85001
(602) 253-6528
Apple

Southeastern Educational
Software
3300 Buckeye Road
Atlanta, GA 30341
(404) 457-8336
Apple

Southern Microsystems For Ed.
P.O. Box 1981
Burlington, NC 27215
(919) 226-7610
Apple II & III, TRS-80 3, IBM

Spinnaker Software
215 First Street
Cambridge, MA 02142
(617) 868-4700

Sterling Swift Publishing Co.
1600 Fortview Rd.
Austin, TX 78704
(512) 444-7570
Apple

Stoneware
50 Belvedere
San Rafael, CA 94901
(415) 454-6500
Apple

Strategic Simulations Inc.
883 Stierlin Road, Bldg. A-200
Mountain View, CA 94043
(415 - 964-1353
Apple, Atari, TRS-80, IBM

SubLOGIC Communications
Corp.
713 Edgebrook Drive
Champaign, IL 61820
(217) 359-8482
Apple, Atari, TRS-80,IBM

Sunburst Communications
P.O. Box 40, 39 Washington Ave.
Pleasantville, NY 10570
(914) 431-1934
Apple, Atari, TRS-80

Sysdata International, Inc.
7671 Old Central Ave., NE
Minneapolis, MN 55432
(612) 780-1750
Apple II

T.H.E.S.I.S.
P.O. Box 147
Garden City, MI 48135
(313) 595-4722
Apple, Atati

TIES
1925 W. County Rd. B2
St. Paul, MN 55113
(612) 633-9100
Apple, Atari

TYC Software
2128 West Jefferson Road
Pittsford, NY 14534
(716) 424-5453
Apple, TRS-80

TYCOM Associates
68 Valma Avenue
Pittsfield, MA 01201
(413) 442-9771
PET

Tamarack Software
P.O. Box 247
Darby, MT 59829
(406) 821-4596
Apple, Atari, PET

Teach Yourself By Computer
Software
2128 W. Jefferson Road
Pittsford, NY 14534
(716) 424-5453
Apple, TRS-80

Teacher's Pet Software
1517 Holly St.
Berkeley, CA 94703
(415) 526-8068
PET

Teaching Pathways, Inc.
P.O. Box 31582
Amarillo, TX 79120
(806) 373-1847
Apple II & III. TRS-80 I & III

Technical Language Systems,
Inc.
P.O. Box 172
San Angelo, TX 76902
(915) 655-0981
Apple

Teck Associates
P.O. Box 8732
White Bear Lake, MN 55110
(612) 429-5570
Apple

Temporal Activity Products Inc.
1535 121st Ave. SE
Bellevue, WA 98005
(206) 746-2790
Apple

Terrapin, Inc.
380 Green Street
Cambridge, MA 02139
(617) 492-8816
Apple

Texas Instruments
P.O. Box 53
Lubbock, TX 79408
(800) 858-4565
TI

The Micro Center
P.O. Box 6
Pleasantville, NY 11801
(516) 796-9392
Apple, Atari, PET, TRS-80

The Professionals Workshop
1 Fletchers Mews, Neath Hill
Milton Keynes, Bucks
England
Apple II

The Programmers, Inc.
P.O Box 1207
Taos, NM 87571
(505) 758-0576
Apple

The Psychological Corp.
757 Third Avenue
New York, NY 10017
(212) 888-3500
Apple, TRS-80

The Upper Room
907 6th Ave. E.
Menomonie, WI 54751
(715) 235-5775
Apple, Texas Instruments

USE, Inc.
14901 E. Hampden Ave., Suite
250
Aurora, CO 80014
(303) 699-0438
Apple, Apple II

Visual Horizons
180 Metro Park
Rochester, NY 14623
(716) 424-5300
Apple

Wadsworth Electronic
Publishing Co.
20 Park Plaza
Boston, MA 02116
(800) 322-2208

Walt Woltosz
655 S. Fair Oaks, M213
Sunnyvale, CA 94086
(408) 733-6358
Apple II, TRS-80